# CORPORATE GOVERNANCE IN SOUTH ASIA

## Trends and Challenges

Authors: Tom Kirchmaier and Carsten Gerner-Beuerle
Edited by: Irum Ahsan and Gregorio Rafael P. Bueta

JANUARY 2021

ASIAN DEVELOPMENT BANK

ADB

# CONTENTS

# TABLES, FIGURE, AND BOX

# FOREWORD

On behalf of the Governance Thematic Group of the of the of the Asian Development Bank (ADB), I would like to congratulate the Law and Policy Reform Program of the Office of the General Counsel and the London School of Economics for this timely and important publication.

Governance matters for sustainable, inclusive, and resilient development. As early as 1995, ADB recognized this and became the first multilateral development bank to adopt a *Governance Policy* to help enhance governance quality in its member countries. Good governance has since then been established as one of the three pillars of ADB's poverty reduction strategy. Its absence, or weakness, hinders the delivery of public services, promotes corruption, and inhibits economic development.[a] Many ADB developing member countries (DMCs) still face governance issues— poor public services, weak government institutions and capacity, and corruption.[b] As emphasized in ADB's Strategy 2030, the region needs governance and institutional reforms to sustain development momentum and ensure that the benefits of growth are equitably and widely shared (footnote 2).

Corporate governance is a theme which cuts across ADB's operations. Good corporate governance, both in the private and public sectors, can help foster long-term sustainable growth. ADB assists countries in bringing corporate governance practices to government institutions, including public service providers, regulatory bodies, and state-owned enterprises (SOEs). Over the years, ADB's work in its DMCs spanned different projects with corporate governance aspects: (i) strengthening overall corporate governance and regulatory frameworks, (ii) reforming capital markets and improving listing requirements, (iii) reorganizing and corporatizing entities, (iv) rationalizing public enterprises, and (v) enhancing the capability of governments to control for corruption.

Work in this space has taken great strides in the last 2 decades. The 1997 Asian financial crisis and the 2008 global financial crisis served as wake-up calls for governments, businesses, investors, and other stakeholders to put in place safeguards that ensure stable markets, mitigate investor and public risks, and improve performance. Today, the coronavirus disease (COVID-19) pandemic once again puts both private and public companies to the test, as lockdowns, restrictions, and health and social concerns

---

[a]  ADB. ADB's Focus on Governance and Public Management. https://www.adb.org/sectors/governance/main.
[b]  ADB. 2019. *Strategy 2030 Operational Plan for Priority 6: Strengthening Governance and Institutional Capacity, 2019–2024.* Manila.

continue with no definite end in sight. The economic and social costs are unprecedented. Of particular concern will be SOEs, many of which supply basic and critical services such as energy, transport, and water to millions in Asia and the Pacific. These SOEs will need significant government financial support and subsidies to keep functioning—and good corporate governance will help ensure that these institutions use the funds judiciously and achieve intended results. Thus, SOEs and corporate governance will play a key role in the recovery process of many countries.

What I described above is just one of the many issues discussed in this publication. The analysis and recommendations—on legal frameworks, board diversity, and compliance and anti-money laundering—point to future trends and reform areas on corporate governance in South Asia. The lessons here can also apply to other regions especially to DMCs. They can serve as a guide for designing projects and interventions by ADB and other development partners, given the ever-changing and complex governance challenges in Asia and the Pacific. This publication also highlights the important role of ADB as a knowledge institution that can share and transfer knowledge and good practices across its DMCs, stakeholders, and to the wider public.

I hope other development practitioners and our partners in government and the private sector find this publication useful. ADB will double its efforts at finding solutions to the governance problems our DMCs face. We look forward to continuing our work and partnership with all of you for improved corporate governance in Asia and the Pacific.

**BRUNO CARRASCO**
Chief of Governance Thematic Group
Asian Development Bank

# FOREWORD

Development—one that is sustainable, inclusive, and resilient—is indeed everybody's business. Government, citizens, civil society, and the private sector must work together to ensure that global development goals are met, especially for the poorest and most vulnerable. Corporations have proved to be a driving force behind the progress of nations, which makes it everybody's business to ensure that corporations are governed fairly and effectively.

Private and financial sector development, which includes corporate governance, is one of the key priority areas under the Asian Development Bank's Law and Policy Reform (LPR) Program. Since 1995, the LPR Program has been supporting the region's economic development through reforms in law and policy. The central premise of the LPR program is that a functioning legal system—anchored by the Rule of Law—is an essential component of meaningful development. Such a system must comprise comprehensive legal frameworks with effective legislative, regulatory, administrative, and judicial institutions that establish, implement, and enforce laws and regulations fairly, consistently, ethically, and predictably.

An economy with such a legal framework, particularly for corporations, respects property rights and contracts, attracts domestic and foreign investment, and encourages growth, thereby creating jobs and generating incomes. If such a framework operates in an environment of inclusiveness with respect to gender and all segments and sectors of society, then it will maximize its potential and effectiveness. Growth will be faster, broader, more stable, and more sustainable.

No doubt corporate governance is crucial for development work around the world. According to the Organisation for Economic Co-operation and Development (OECD), good corporate governance practices cannot develop without appropriate public policy, without an adequate legal and regulatory framework.[a] The International Finance Corporation (IFC) notes that better-governed corporate frameworks benefit firms through greater access to financing, lower cost of capital, better firm performance, and more favorable treatment of all stakeholders - when a country's overall corporate governance and property rights systems are weak, voluntary and market corporate governance mechanisms have more limited effectiveness.[b]

---

[a]  S. Nestor, T. Yasui, and M. Guy. The Relevance of Corporate Governance to Eurasian Transition Economies. OECD. https://www.oecd.org/corporate/ca/corporategovernanceprinciples/1930716.pdf.

[b]  S. Claessens and B. Yurtoglu. 2012. Corporate Governance and Development – AN Update. IFC. https://www.ifc.org/wps/wcm/connect/15fae179-97e0-48ea-a123-abc07deabd36/Focus10_CG%26Development.pdf?MOD=AJPERES&CVID=jtCwukM.

This Report talks about: (i) the challenges facing corporate governance not just in South Asia but in the rest of the world; (ii) how corporate governance legal frameworks continue to evolve, especially with the rising scrutiny not only from investors but from shareholders and other stakeholders too; and (iii) the importance of well-managed, independent, structured, and diverse boards. This Report also highlights that in many developing countries, state-owned enterprises are a key part of the economy and in critical sectors such as energy and finance – thus making their governance a priority for development reform. Lastly, anti-money laundering and compliance issues are also important considerations in corporate governance to ensure the public's trust and confidence in these institutions.

This Report is a result of ADB's collaboration with the South Asian Association for Regional Cooperation in Law (SAARCLAW) to look at legal and regulatory issues in South Asia. We thank SAARCLAW and its leadership for the fruitful partnership and meaningful interaction on issues such as corporate governance and energy trade.

In this note, I want to acknowledge the Report authors, Thomas Kirchmaier of the London School of Economics, and Carsten Gerner-Buerle of University College London for the excellent discussions and insights in the pages that follow. The country reports were prepared with the assistance of Natalia Bilimoria, University College London, United Kingdom; Saqeb Mahbub, Mahbub & Company, Dhaka, Bangladesh; and Faiz Ullah Khan Niazi, University College London, United Kingdom. I would also like to thank Gregorio Rafael P. Bueta for helping me in editing and publishing the Report.

This Report focuses mainly on countries in South Asia, but the lessons and learnings are very relevant for other regions, especially for many developing countries around the world. Corporate governance will continue to be an essential part of the law and policy space, especially with evolving challenges brought about by the COVID-19 pandemic, climate change, and sustainable global trade, just to name a few. We hope that this Report contributes to finding solutions to these issues. May it also inspire ideas and actions of development practitioners for the critical work ahead.

**IRUM AHSAN**
Project Leader and Advisor, Office of the Compliance Review Panel
Asian Development Bank

# ABBREVIATIONS

| | | |
|---|---|---|
| AML | – | anti-money laundering |
| AMLA | – | Asset (Money) Laundering Act (Nepal) |
| AMLA | – | Anti-Money Laundering Act (Pakistan) |
| APG | – | Asia/Pacific Group on Money Laundering |
| BFIU | – | Bangladesh Financial Intelligence Unit |
| BSEC | – | Bangladesh Securities and Exchange Commission |
| CAG | – | Comptroller and Auditor General |
| CEO | – | chief executive officer |
| CSE | – | Colombo Stock Exchange |
| CTF | – | counter-terror finance (financing) |
| DNFBP | – | designated nonfinancial businesses and professions |
| FATF | – | Financial Action Task Force |
| FTRA | – | Financial Transactions Reporting Act |
| FIU | – | financial intelligence unit |
| GDP | – | gross domestic product |
| HR&R | – | human resources and remuneration |
| IFC | – | International Finance Corporation |
| LOD | – | line of defense |
| MER | – | mutual evaluation report |
| MLPA | – | Money Laundering Prevention Act |
| NRC | – | Nomination and Remuneration Committee |
| OECD | – | Organisation for Economic Co-operation and Development |
| PE | – | public enterprise |
| PAC | – | Public Accounts Committee |
| PMLA | – | Prevention of Money Laundering Act (Sri Lanka) |
| SAARC | – | South Asian Association for Regional Cooperation |
| SAR | – | Suspicious Activity Report |
| STR | – | Suspicious Transaction Report |
| SOE | – | state-owned enterprise |
| UAPA | – | Unlawful Activities (Prevention) Act |
| UK | – | United Kingdom |
| US | – | United States |

# BACKGROUND

Strong corporate governance institutions, both in the form of "hard" law and "soft" law, are important to attract foreign direct investment as well as portfolio investment. They facilitate the growth of capital markets and economic development, in general.[a] It is widely argued that companies with a good corporate governance system have better financial performance.[b] This is important as it helps to lower the real costs of capital, a key cornerstone for the creation of wealth in a nation.

## Corporate Governance in South Asia

In South Asia, important steps have been taken over the last 15 years toward the improvement of national regulatory frameworks and the development of effective corporate governance structures, driven partly by (i) international initiatives such as the Organisation for Economic Co-operation and Development (OECD)–Asian Roundtable on Corporate Governance, which set out an ambitious reform program in its 2003 white paper on corporate governance in Asia, and the World Bank, which monitors the implementation of international standards on corporate governance,[c] partly by international financial institutions that have devised, under the auspices of the International Finance Corporation (IFC), a common methodology for assessing corporate governance in investee companies;[d] and by (ii) national government bodies and private sector associations.[e]

## About this Report

This report has been prepared under the ADB project *Strengthening Legal Institutions and Enhancing Regional Cooperation in Law, Justice, and Development in the South Asian Association for Regional Cooperation Region*. Under this technical assistance (TA), work was initiated based on the memorandum of understanding between ADB, through the Law and Policy Reform Program of the

---

[a] World Bank. 2017. Doing Business 2017: Equal Opportunity for All, Washington, DC.; S. Claessens and B. Yurtoglu. 2012. Corporate Governance and Development—An Update. IFC Focus 10.

[b] K.J. Lee. 2020. The Effects of Privatization and Corporate Governance of SOEs in Transition Economy: The Case of Kazakhstan. *ADB Institute (ADBI) Working Paper 1127*. Tokyo: ADBI. p. 6. https://www.adb.org/publications/privatization-corporategovernance-soes-transition-economy-kazakhstan.

[c] World Bank, Reports on the Observance of Standards and Codes (ROSC). The ROSC initiative benchmarks a country's corporate governance framework and company practices against the G20/OECD Principles for Corporate Governance and provides assistance with a view to strengthening institutional capacity. ROSC country reports are available at http://documents.worldbank.org/curated/en/docsearch/document-type/904559.

[d] IFC. Corporate Governance Development Framework. http://cgdevelopmentframework.com/cg-development-framework.

[e] See Chapter 1, Table 1.

Office of the General Counsel, and the South Asian Association for Regional Cooperation in Law (SAARCLAW). One of the objectives of the TA was to work on legal and regulatory reform and cooperation in South Asia, through SAARCLAW and the legal community in the region. This was done under the project's three components: (i) developing capacity on legal and regulatory harmonization for regional integration, (ii) developing and disseminating knowledge products on priority legal and regulatory issues, and (iii) institutional strengthening through a permanent secretariat.

Corporate governance was one of the areas of reform identified under this project. To begin this work, ADB, in collaboration with the London School of Economics, IFC, the Financial Times, the Governance Thematic Group and the Private Sector Operations Department organized a workshop on **Corporate Governance in Asia and the Pacific** at ADB headquarters in November 2017. This important conference built on ADB's extensive work, both with the private and state-owned enterprises (SOEs), to enhance corporate governance. The premise was that institutionalizing best practices in corporate governance will strengthen companies and attract greater investment. Over 100 regulators, judges, corporate executives, lawyers, and ADB staff deliberated on issues relating to corporate governance and best practices in private enterprises and SOEs. Some of the topics discussed include: corporate governance codes and scorecards, shareholder activism, board diversity (particularly gender diverse boards), SOE reforms, and dealing with corporate scandals. The conference highlighted the need for continued capacity development work in this area, especially in South Asia.

This knowledge product, prepared in collaboration with the London School of Economics, looks at several corporate governance issues from the South Asian Association for Regional Cooperation (SAARC) regional perspective and provides an analysis in light of global trends and best practices. The report provides an analytical overview of the state of play in four core areas of corporate governance in South Asia in order to assess whether the necessary regulatory preconditions for strong financial and economic development are in place, and identify areas for further regulatory action. Chapter 1 discusses the general regulatory framework on corporate governance, including both codes of best practice and relevant requirements laid down in the binding company legislation or in listing rules. Chapter 2 gives a more detailed account of best practice standards and regulatory requirements concerning board structure and board diversity, in particular gender diversity. Chapter 3 analyzes the corporate governance regime applicable to SOEs, whose role in South Asian economies is substantial, representing 10%–15% of gross domestic product in most economies. Chapter 4 evaluates anti-money laundering legislation and initiatives combating financial crime.

Each chapter contains country reports for a subset of more economically developed SAARC member countries with robust corporate law and practice (Bangladesh, Nepal, Pakistan, and Sri Lanka). The appendix reproduces relevant laws and regulations in India, the region's biggest economy, for comparative purposes. The country reports are followed by a critical assessment of the robustness and effectiveness of the national frameworks—benchmarked, where appropriate, against the laws and best practice standards of countries whose regulatory framework has become a template for the international development of best practice standards and/or where historical links exist to the laws of the SAARC member countries examined here. Where shortcomings are identified, we make recommendations on how these can be rectified.

# CORPORATE GOVERNANCE FRAMEWORKS

## Introduction

Corporate governance is typically regulated by a combination of hard law,[1] binding provisions in company legislation regulating the basic governance architecture of companies, directors' duties, shareholder rights and minority shareholder protection mechanisms; and soft law,[2] best practice standards set out in corporate governance codes. This trend toward a more flexible regulation of the conflicts of interest prevalent in corporations began in the United States in the early 1970s with statements regarding the role and responsibilities of directors issued by the Business Roundtable, the National Association of Corporate Directors, and the Council of Institutional Investors.[3] Since then, private organizations, stock exchanges, and some large institutional investors or associations of investors in most developed and developing economies have produced increasingly detailed sets of best practice standards containing provisions on board composition, independence requirements for outside directors, committees of the board, and the role of shareholders. In some countries, these standards have been incorporated into the listing rules of stock exchanges and are, accordingly, binding on companies listed in prime market segment;[4] in others they operate on a comply-or-explain basis.

Corporate governance codes exist in most, but not all, member countries of the South Asian Association for Regional Cooperation (SAARC). Table 1 gives an overview of the most recent initiatives.

---

[1]   Acts of Parliament, decree laws, regulations, etc. that cannot be misapplied by the parties.
[2]   Instruments without binding legal force.
[3]   See, for example, Business Roundtable. 1978. The Role and Composition of the Board of Directors of the Large Publicly Owned Corporation. 33 Business Lawyer 2083.
[4]   See, for example, Section 303A of the Listed Company Manual of the New York Stock Exchange.

### Table 1: Corporate Governance Codes in SAARC Member Countries

| Country | Code | Issuer | Latest Edition |
|---|---|---|---|
| Afghanistan | None | | |
| Bangladesh | Corporate Governance Code[a]<br>Code of Corporate Governance for Bangladesh[b] | Bangladesh Securities and Exchange Commission<br>Bangladesh Enterprise Institute | 2018<br>2004 |
| Bhutan | None | | |
| India | Corporate Governance Voluntary Guidelines[c]<br>Corporate Governance Recommendations | Ministry of Corporate Affairs<br>Confederation of Indian Industry | 2009<br>2009 |
| Maldives | Corporate Governance Code[d] | Capital Market Development Authority | 2014 |
| Nepal | None | | |
| Pakistan | Code of Corporate Governance[e] | Securities and Exchange Commission of Pakistan | 2019 |
| Sri Lanka | Code of Best Practice on Corporate Governance[f] | Institute of Chartered Accountants /Securities and Exchange Commission of Sri Lanka | 2017 |

SAARC = South Asian Association for Regional Cooperation.

[a] Bangladesh Securities and Exchange Commission. 2018. *Corporate Governance Code*. 3 June. https://www.sec.gov.bd/slaws/Corporate_Governance_Code_10.06.2018.pdf.

[b] Bangladesh Enterprise Institute. 2004. *The Code of Corporate Governance for Bangladesh*. http://bei-bd.org/wp-content/uploads/2015/03/whc4f4b6d540eb13.pdf.

[c] Government of India, Ministry of Corporate Affairs. *Corporate Governance Voluntary Guidelines 2009*. https://www.mca.gov.in/Ministry/latestnews/CG_Voluntary_Guidelines_2009_24dec2009.pdf.

[d] Capital Market Development Authority. *Corporate Governance Code* (last amended 14 January 2014). https://www.cmda.gov.mv/assets/Laws-and-Regulations/Code-Coporate-Governance/Corporate-Governace-CodeJan-2014-English-Searchable.pdf.

[e] Government of Pakistan, Securities and Exchange Commission of Pakistan. Listed Companies *Code of Corporate Governance* Regulations 2019. https://www.secp.gov.pk/document/listed-companies-code-of-corporate-governance-regulations-2019/?wpdmdl=36088.

[f] Institute of Chartered Accountants of Sri Lanka. *Code of Best Practice on Corporate Governance 2017*. Colombo. https://www.casrilanka.com/casl/images/stories/2017/2017_pdfs/code_of_best_practice_on_corporate_governance_2017_final_for_web.pdf.

Source: Asian Development Bank.

## Corporate Governance and Financial/Economic Development in South Asia

The goal of corporate governance, according to the World Bank and most national policy makers, is the protection of minority investors. The World Bank Doing Business reports measure good governance as an aggregate of six elements: (i) review, approval, and disclosure of requirements for related-party transactions; (ii) ability of minority shareholders to sue and hold interested directors liable for prejudicial related-party transactions; (iii) ease of filing a minority shareholder lawsuit (derivative action), (iv) shareholder rights in major corporate transactions, (v) governance safeguards protecting shareholders from undue board control and entrenchment, and (vi) extent of corporate transparency.[5] The World Bank has carried out an assessment of the four SAARC economies that are the focus of this study along these dimensions with the results summarized in Table 2.

The following country sections build on the World Bank's analysis, with certain modifications: the scope of this publication is narrower, focusing on the regulatory framework governing the general management of companies, as opposed to fundamental transactions. At the same time, a more granular and detailed analysis is offered, considering, for example, the precise structure of directors' duties or the content of best practice standards where this is relevant to an evaluation of the effectiveness of corporate governance codes, such as the definition of independence. Finally, it considers how the relevant provisions are enforced in practice and offer a view on the law "in action", including, where applicable, leading case law.

As far as best practice standards are concerned, it records (i) the proportion of nonexecutive to executive directors on the board; (ii) the number of independent directors; (iii) the definition of independence; (iv) the separation of the two central roles on the board, that of chair and chief executive officer (CEO); (v) the delegation of sensitive issues involving particularly pronounced conflicts of interest to independent committees, including succession planning, responsibility for the review of internal control procedures and the appointment of the external auditor, and remuneration decisions; and (vi) the mechanisms facilitating the enforcement of best practice standards.[6]

### Table 2: Minority Investor Protection Index (0-10)

| Dimension | Bangladesh | Nepal | Pakistan | Sri Lanka |
|---|---|---|---|---|
| Related-party transactions | 6 | 6 | 6 | 8 |
| Liability of directors | 7 | 1 | 7 | 5 |
| Ease of filing a shareholder lawsuit | 7 | 9 | 6 | 7 |
| Shareholder rights | 5 | 7 | 8 | 7 |
| Governance safeguards | 3 | 6 | 9 | 6 |
| Corporate transparency | 5 | 6 | 7 | 7 |
| Country rank (out of 190) | 89 | 72 | 26 | 38 |

Source: World Bank Doing Business 2019.

---

[5]   In addition, detailed methodologies exist to measure corporate governance at the firm level. See, for example, the framework developed by IFC, which has been adopted by 35 development finance institutions, including ADB. For a detailed description of the framework, see IFC. Corporate Governance Development Framework. http://cgdevelopmentframework.com/cg-development-framework .

[6]   Other countries have been analyzed along these six dimensions in C. Gerner-Beuerle. 2017. Diffusion of Regulatory Innovations: The Case of Corporate Governance Codes.13 *Journal of Institutional Economics 271.*

These best practice standards have to be assessed against the backdrop of the binding legal and general institutional system. Hence, the country reports also evaluate (i) the legal rights of shareholders to appoint and remove directors, (ii) the structure of directors' duties, (iii) the enforcement of these duties by minority shareholders on behalf of the company, and (iv) the nonlegal institutional determinants of the effectiveness of the above. Other complementary or functionally equivalent regulatory institutions, for example, disclosure regulation and the activities and powers of public regulatory bodies, are outside the scope of this study.

# National Approaches

## *Bangladesh*

### Overview of the Regulatory Framework

Companies are incorporated and regulated by the Companies Act, 1994. The act is supplemented by a Corporate Governance Code, the most recent edition issued in 2018 by the Bangladesh Securities and Exchange Commission (BSEC). The code does not operate on a "comply-or-explain" basis, but is binding on all companies falling within its remit. It was published by the BSEC by virtue of its authority to "impose conditions" under s. 2CC of the Securities and Exchange Ordinance, 1969. Although the code itself does not mention penalties for noncompliance, the Securities and Exchange Ordinance, 1969, s. 22(b) contains penalties for noncompliance with an order or direction of the BSEC. No "explain" provision is found in the code.

Government regulators for corporate governance in Bangladesh are the Registrar of Joint Stock Companies and Firms, the BSEC, and Bangladesh Bank, the central bank of Bangladesh. Nongovernment regulators are the Institute of Chartered Accountants of Bangladesh, Chittagong Stock Exchange, and Dhaka Stock Exchange.

### Board Structure

Table 3 gives an overview of the regulation of corporate boards in Bangladesh along the five dimensions that section 1.2 identified as critical in ensuring that boards operate as an effective, independent control mechanism. The table also gives information on the manner in which the regulatory requirements are enforced, in particular whether companies can deviate from them, provided they give an explanation of their noncompliance; or the board structure framework is laid down in binding regulations. The provisions are contained in the Corporate Governance Code, 2018.

**Table 3: Board Structure Regulation in Bangladesh**

| Dimension | Regulatory Requirements Applicable to Listed Companies | Summary |
|---|---|---|
| Proportion of nonexecutive directors | No distinction between executive and nonexecutive directors (but see the requirements on independence, which implicitly establish a minimum percentage of nonexecutive directors) | No minimum proportion |
| Number of independent directors | Condition no. 1(2)(a) of the Corporate Governance Code, 2018: At least one-fifth of the total number of directors on the company's board shall be independent directors. | One-fifth |
| Definition of independence | Condition no. 1(2) of the Corporate Governance Code, 2018: "independent director" means a director:<br>• who either does not hold any share in the company or holds **less than 1% share** of the total paid-up shares of the company;<br>• who is not a **sponsor** of the company or is not connected with any sponsor of the company or director or nominated director or shareholder of the company or any of its associates, sister concerns, subsidiaries, and parents or holding entities on the basis of **family relationships**, and his or her family members also shall not hold abovementioned shares in the company;<br>• who has not been an **executive** of the company in immediately preceding 2 financial years;<br>• who does not have **any other relationship**, whether pecuniary or otherwise, with the company or its subsidiary or associated companies;<br>• who is not a member or a Trading Right Entitlement Certificate (TREC) holder, director, or officer **of any stock exchange**;<br>• who is not a shareholder, director (excepting independent director), or officer of any member or TREC holder of any stock exchange or an **intermediary of the capital market**;<br>• who is not a partner or an executive or was not a partner or an executive during the preceding 3 years of the concerned company's **statutory audit firm**;<br>• who is not an independent director in **more than five listed companies**;<br>• who has not been convicted by a court of competent jurisdiction as a **defaulter** in payment of any loan or any advance to a bank or a nonbank financial institution; and<br>• who has not been convicted for a **criminal offense** involving moral turpitude. | Detailed and demanding definition |
| Separation of chair and CEO | Condition no. 1(4)(a) of the Corporate Governance Code, 2018: The roles of the chair of the board and CEO have to be separated and held by different individuals. | Required |
| Committee structure | **Succession planning:** The board must set up a Nomination and Remuneration Committee (NRC) to assist the board in the formulation of nomination criteria or the policy for determining qualifications, positive attributes, experiences and independence of directors and top-level executive, as well as a policy for considering the remuneration of directors and top-level executives (condition no. 6 of the Corporate Governance Code). The NRC must comprise of at least three members who must all be nonexecutive directors, including at least one independent director.<br>**Audit:** The board must establish an audit committee that shall monitor the internal audit and compliance process, review the internal audit and compliance report, and oversee the hiring and performance of the external auditors (condition no. 5 of the Corporate Governance Code).<br>The audit committee must be composed of at least three members who must be nonexecutive directors (excepting the chair of the board) and include at least one independent director. In addition, all members must be financially literate and at least one member must have accounting or related financial management background and 10 years of such experience.<br>**Remuneration:** See above, succession planning | Nomination: yes<br>Audit: yes<br>Remuneration: yes |
| Enforcement | Binding on listed companies | Compliance mandatory |

Source: Authors.

**Further Minority Protection Mechanisms**

*Appointment and Removal of Directors*

According to s. 91 of the Companies Act, 1994, the directors of a company are elected by the shareholders from among them in general meeting. Section 106 of the Companies Act, 1994 provides that a company may, by extraordinary resolution, remove any shareholder-director before the expiration of his or her period of office with or without cause, and may, by ordinary resolution, appoint another person in the same position.

*Directors' Duties*

The Companies Act, 1994 does not lay down the duties of a director. However, the act contains a number of provisions aimed at checking the neglect of duties by a director, and a breach of these provisions will entail liability. In particular:

- s. 104 prohibits a director from holding any office of profit under the company except that of a managing director, manager, or a legal or technical adviser or banker.
- s. 105 provides that except with the consent of the directors, a director of a company, or the firm of which he is a partner, or any partner of such firm or the private company of which he is a director or member, shall not enter into any contract for the sale, purchase, or supply of goods and materials of the company.

*Related-Party Transactions*

The Companies Act, 1994 requires related-party transactions to be disclosed and interested directors to abstain from voting on such transactions. More specifically, s. 130 provides that a director, who is directly or indirectly concerned or interested in a contract or arrangement entered into by or on behalf of the company, must disclose the nature of his or her interest at the meeting of the directors dealing with the contract or arrangement (a general notice that a director is a director or a member of any specified company or of a specified firm, and is to be regarded as interested in any subsequent transaction with that firm or company, is sufficient). The company must keep a register of all transactions with a director, which must be open to inspection by any member of the company.

Further, pursuant to s. 131, directors must abstain from voting on any contract or arrangement in which they are directly or indirectly interested, and their presence does not count for the purpose of forming a quorum.

*Minority Shareholder Lawsuits*

The Companies Act, 1994 provides for certain functions to be undertaken by the shareholders, such as attending meetings, appointing and removing directors, and exercising their right to obtain financial information, as well as approving annually the balance sheet. The law also provides for certain mechanisms for shareholders to enforce these rights, the principal among them being a suit for minority protection under s. 233 of the act. According to s. 233, members or debenture holders of a company may lodge an application with the High Court claiming that:

a. the affairs of the company are being conducted or the powers of the directors are being exercised in a manner prejudicial to one or more of its members or debenture holders, or in disregard of his or her, or their interest;

b.  the company is acting or is likely to act in a manner which discriminated or is likely to discriminate against the interest of any member or debenture holder; or

c.  a resolution of the members, debenture holders, or any class of them has been passed or is likely to be passed, which discriminates or is likely to discriminate against the interest of one or more of the members or debenture holders.

The minority suit can be brought by shareholders holding at least 10% of the shares issued. Upon application by the minority shareholders, if the High Court is of the view that the interest of the minority shareholders are being prejudicially affected, it has the power to make the following orders: (i) cancel or modify any resolution or transaction, (ii) regulate the affairs of the company to ensure that the order of the court is being enforced, or (iii) amend any provision of the memorandum or articles of the company.

Although minority shareholders are given protection under s. 233, the provision has remained of limited relevance. Shareholders are often not aware of s. 233 and the minority protection regime. In addition, the holding of a minimum 10% of the issued shares to file an application constitutes a significant barrier to minority protection. Further, the application under s. 233 can only be moved in the Company Bench of the High Court, where legal costs are generally high. The effectiveness of the minority protection regime is further called into question by the fact that the judiciary suffers from considerable backlogs and cases are often pending for several months before a hearing.

## *Nepal*

### Overview of the Regulatory Framework

Companies are governed by the Companies Act, 2063 (2006), as well as sector-specific acts, notably the Bank and Financial Institutions Act, 2073 (2017); Securities Act, 2063 (2007); and Insurance Act, 2049 (1992). A corporate governance code or best practice standards has not been adopted outside of the financial sector in Nepal. However, the Securities Board of Nepal, Nepal Rastra Bank, and the Insurance Board—the three regulators for the capital markets, banking, and the insurance sector respectively—have issued directives dealing with certain aspects of corporate governance. Relevant for present purposes is in particular the Securities Board of Nepal Listed Companies Corporate Governance Directive, 2074 (2018), which, among other issues, limits the maximum tenure of a director to 4 years, prohibits the appointment of more than one director from the same family, requires the position of chair of the board and CEO to be separated, stipulates that listed companies shall establish a risk management committee, and strengthens transparency.

### Board Structure

Table 4 gives an overview of the regulation of corporate boards in Nepal along the five dimensions that section 1.2 identified as critical in ensuring that boards operate as an effective, independent control mechanism, as well as the manner in which the regulatory requirements are enforced. The provisions are to be found in the binding companies legislation, the Companies Act, 2063 (2006), unless otherwise indicated.

## Table 4: Board Structure Regulation in Nepal

| Dimension | Regulatory Requirements Applicable to Listed Companies | Summary |
|---|---|---|
| Proportion of nonexecutive directors | No distinction between executive and nonexecutive directors (but see the requirements on independence) | No minimum proportion |
| Number of independent directors | s. 86(3) Companies Act 2006: if the board is composed of not more than seven directors, at least one independent director, and if the board is composed of more than seven directors, at least two independent directors, must be appointed from among the persons who have the knowledge as prescribed in the articles of association of the company, and gained knowledge and experience in the business of the company concerned. | One or two |
| Definition of independence | s. 89 Companies Act 2006: Persons who are not eligible to be appointed as independent directors include anyone:<br>• who is below the **age of 21**;<br>• who is a **declared insolvent** and a period of 5 years has not lapsed;<br>• who is **convicted of certain offenses** (corruption, theft, fraud, forgery, and embezzlement or misuse of goods or funds entrusted to him or her);<br>• who has a **personal interest** of any kind in the business or any contract or transaction of the concerned company;<br>• who is already a director, substantial shareholder, employee, auditor, or adviser of **another company having similar objectives** or has a personal interest of any kind in such company;<br>• who is holding the office of director receiving from **another listed company** any remuneration or facility, other than a meeting allowance and actual expenses incurred;<br>• who is a **shareholder** of the concerned company;<br>• who has not obtained at least a bachelor's degree in a subject that is related to the business to be carried on by the concerned company and gained at least **10 years of experience** in the related field or in the management of company affairs, or who has not obtained at least a bachelor's degree in finance, economics, management, accounts, statistics, commerce, trade, or law and gained at least 10 years of experience in the related field;<br>• who is an **officer, auditor, or employee** of the concerned company or a period of 3 years has not lapsed after his/her retirement from any such office;<br>• who is the **close relative** of the office of the concerned company; and<br>• who is an **auditor** of the concerned company. | Detailed and demanding definition |
| Separation of chair and chief executive officer (CEO) | Listed Companies Corporate Governance Directive, 2074: holding the position of both chair and CEO in the same company is prohibited. | Required |
| Committee structure | **Succession planning:** Not required.<br>**Audit:** Pursuant to s. 164 Companies Act 2006, a listed company with paid-up capital of NRs30 million or more, or a company which is fully or partly owned by the Government of Nepal, shall form an audit committee under the chairpersonship of a director, who is not involved in the day-to-day operations of the company, and consisting of at least three members.<br>A person who is a close relative of the chief executive of a company shall not be eligible to be a member of the audit committee.<br>At least one member of the audit committee must be an experienced person having obtained a professional certificate on accounting, or a person having gained experience in accounting and finance after having obtained at least bachelor's degree in accounting, commerce, management, finance, or economics.<br>**Remuneration:** Not required (but note that the general meeting decides on the remuneration of directors pursuant to ss. 77(6), 91 Companies Act 2006. | Nomination: no<br>Audit: yes<br>Remuneration: no |
| Enforcement | The above requirements are not best practice rules, but binding requirements. | Compliance mandatory |

Source: Authors.

## Further Minority Protection Mechanisms

### Appointment and Removal of Directors

Directors are appointed by the general meeting of the company (Companies Act 2006, s. 87[1]). They may be removed by ordinary resolution of the general meeting with or without cause (Companies Act 2006, s. 89[3][b]).

### Directors' Duties

Pursuant to s. 95(2), directors of a public company must not derive any personal benefit through the company, except in accordance with a decision of the general meeting. The company may recover damages from a director for any loss caused to the company from an act beyond the director's jurisdiction (s. 95[4]).

Section 99 Companies Act 2006 sets out further duties of directors in more detail.

First, the provision reiterates that directors must avoid deriving a personal benefit through the company or in the course of conducting business of the company. If a director has derived a personal benefit in contravention of this section, the company can recover the amount from the director as if it was a loan.

Second, every director and officer of a company must, in discharging their duties, act honestly and in good faith, having regard to the interest and benefit of the company; and exercise such care, caution, wisdom, diligence, and efficiency as a reasonable and prudent person would exercise. Again, the company has a right to recover damages for any loss or damage caused by a director who acts with an ulterior motive in contravention of this provision.

Finally, directors have a duty to comply with the Companies Act, memorandum of association, and articles of association of the company.

### Related-Party Transactions

Transactions between associated companies must be disclosed to the shareholders pursuant to s. 175 Companies Act 2006. Associated companies are defined as a company and its holding company, a company and any subsidiary of its holding company, a subsidiary of the company and its holding company, and a subsidiary of the company and another subsidiary of its holding company (s. 175[1]). Further, directors and their partners or proxies are precluded from voting on any discussion held at any general meeting in respect of the responsibility for an act done or omitted to be done or done wrongfully by them, or in respect of any agreement, contract, or arrangement regarding their employment or anything in which their interest or concern are involved (s. 70[2]).

As far as the position of directors *qua* director is concerned, the following requirements apply: directors who have an interest directly or indirectly linked to any kind of contract, lease, transaction, or agreement entered into with the director's company or a subsidiary, have to disclose the matter promptly to the company, setting out the extent and kind of the interest (s. 92[4]).

Pursuant to s. 93(1), a public company is prohibited from entering into any "significant transaction" with its director, or his or her close relative, or substantial shareholder without approval of the general meeting. Likewise, a subsidiary company is prohibited from entering into any significant transaction with a director (or a close relative or substantial shareholder) of the holding company without approval of the general meeting of the holding company. Significant transaction is defined as a transaction the value of which exceeds NRs100,000 or 5% of the total assets of the company, whichever is the lesser. However, transactions that are carried out at the prevailing market price in the ordinary course of business transaction of the company (s. 93[3][c]) are excluded from the approval requirement.

In the case of a contravention of s. 93(1), any amount or benefit derived directly or indirectly from the transaction must be returned to the company; and if any loss or damage has been incurred by the company, the person deriving a benefit from the transaction is required to pay compensation for the loss (s. 93[2]).

### Minority Shareholder Lawsuits

The Companies Act provides for several procedural mechanisms designed to protect minority shareholders.

First, pursuant to s. 138 Companies Act 2006, any shareholder may make a petition to the court to prevent a director or officer of the company from acting *ultra vires*.

Second, pursuant to s.139, if the business of a company is carried on in a manner prejudicial to the rights and interests of any shareholder, or an act done on behalf of the company has resulted in a prejudice to the rights and interests of any shareholder, the shareholder may make a complaint to the court for an appropriate order. The petitioning shareholder must prove that the director or manager has acted with an ulterior motive or discriminatory, in contravention of the memorandum of association, articles of association, or a shareholder agreement. If the petition is successful, the court may issue such order as it deems fit, for example, an injunction preventing an act from being taken or requiring the company to perform a specified act, requiring the instigation of a civil case on behalf of the company, the buyout of a shareholder, or payment of compensation to a shareholder or to the company.

Third, s. 140(2) provides that if the company fails to enforce a claim it has against a director, officer, or shareholder, any shareholder holding 2.5% or more of the shares in the paid-up capital of the company may file a claim on behalf of the company against the director, officer, or controller separately or jointly with two or more shareholders holding 5% of the share capital. If the claim made by the claimant shareholder is sustained, the legal expenses incurred by him or her shall be reimbursed by the company. If the claim is not sustained, such amount out of the expenses incurred by the defendant as the court thinks appropriate must be reimbursed by the claimant shareholder.

## Pakistan

### Overview of the Regulatory Framework

The Listed Companies (Code of Corporate Governance) Regulations, 2019 (hereinafter referred to as the 2019 Code), contains the currently applicable corporate governance code. It was adopted by the Securities and Exchange Commission of Pakistan (SECP), pursuant to the powers conferred on it by s. 156 and s. 512 of the Companies Act, 2017. The 2019 Code is applicable to all listed companies in Pakistan, and all other entities where the statutes and underlying licensing requirements require such entities to comply with the 2019 Code. The code contains both mandatory provisions and provisions that operate on a comply-or-explain principle. In the former case, noncompliance will entail a financial penalty under reg. 37 of the 2019 Code and s. 512(2) of the Companies Act, 2017. In the latter case, the company is required to provide an appropriate explanation in its statement of compliance, which has to be published together with the company's annual report (2019 Code, reg. 36[1]).

## Board Structure

Table 5 gives an overview of the regulation of corporate boards in Pakistan along the five dimensions that section 1.2 identified as critical in ensuring that boards operate as an effective, independent control mechanism, as well as the manner in which the regulatory requirements are enforced. The requirements are laid down mostly in the 2019 Code, while certain additional provisions, in particular concerning the independence of directors, have been included in the binding companies legislation, the Companies Act, 2017.

### Table 5: Board Structure Regulation in Pakistan

| Dimension | Regulatory Requirements Applicable to Listed Companies | Summary |
|---|---|---|
| Proportion of nonexecutive directors | 2019 Code, reg. 8(1): It is mandatory that the executive directors, including the chief executive officer (CEO), shall not be more than one-third of the board. | Two-thirds |
| Number of independent directors | 2019 Code, reg. 6(1): It is mandatory that each listed company shall have at least two-thirds or one-third of the members of the board, whichever is higher, as independent directors. | One-third |
| Definition of independence | Companies Act, 2017, s. 166(2): An independent director means a director who is not connected or does not have any relationship, whether pecuniary or otherwise, with the company, its associated companies, subsidiaries, holding company or directors; and can be reasonably perceived as being able to exercise independent business judgment without being subservient to any form of conflict of interest. No director shall be considered independent if one or more of the following circumstances exist: <br>• has been an **employee** of the company, any of its subsidiaries or holding company within the last 3 years; <br>• has been the **CEO** of subsidiaries, associated company, associated undertaking or holding company in the last 3 years; <br>• has had within the last 3 years a **material business relationship** with the company either directly, or indirectly as a partner, major shareholder (i.e., holding 10% or more of the share capital), or director of a body that has such a relationship with the company; <br>• has received remuneration in the 3 years preceding appointment as a director or receives **additional remuneration**, excluding retirement benefits from the company apart from a director's fee, or has participated in the company's stock option or a performance-related pay scheme; <br>• is a **close relative** of the company's promoters, directors, or major shareholders; <br>• holds **cross-directorships** or has significant links with other directors through involvement in other companies or bodies not being the associations licensed under section 42 (not-for-profit company); <br>• has served on the board for more than **three consecutive terms**; and <br>• a person nominated as a director under sections 164 and 165 (a director nominated by the company's creditors or other special interests by virtue of contractual arrangements). | Detailed and demanding definition |
| Separation of chair and CEO | 2019 Code, reg. 9(1) (nonmandatory): The chair and CEO of a company, by whatever name called, shall not be the same person. | Required |

*continued on next page*

*Table 5 continued*

| Dimension | Regulatory Requirements Applicable to Listed Companies | Summary |
|---|---|---|
| Committee structure | **Succession planning:** Pursuant to reg. 29(1) of the 2019 Code (nonmandatory), the board may establish a nomination committee, of such number and class of directors, as it may deem appropriate in the circumstances.<br>**Audit:** Pursuant to reg. 27(1) of the 2019 Code (mandatory), the board must establish an audit committee of at least three members comprising of nonexecutive directors and at least one independent director. The chair of the committee shall be an independent director, who shall not be the chair of the board, and at least one member of the audit committee must be financially literate.<br>**Remuneration:** Pursuant to reg. 28(1) and (2) of the 2019 Code (nonmandatory), the board shall establish a human resource and remuneration committee of at least three members comprising a majority of nonexecutive directors, of whom at least one member shall be an independent director. The chair of the committee must be an independent director and the CEO may be included as a member of the committee. In addition, pursuant to reg. 30(1) of the 2019 Code (nonmandatory), the board may establish a **Risk Management Committee**, of such number and class of directors, as it may deem appropriate in the circumstances, to carry out a review of effectiveness of risk management procedures and present a report to the board. | Nomination: yes (nonmandatory) Audit: yes (mandatory) Remuneration: yes (nonmandatory) |
| Enforcement | Mandatory provisions are designated as such in the code. Other provisions are comply-or-explain. | Largely mandatory |

Source: Authors.

## Further Minority Protection Mechanisms

### Appointment and Removal of Directors

Section 159 of the Companies Act, 2017 sets out the procedure for the election of directors. Within 35 days before the general meeting, the existing directors of the company shall fix the number of directors to be elected (s. 159[1]). The directors are elected by the members of the company in general meeting (s. 159[2]). Each member shall have such a number of votes as is equal to the product of the number of voting shares or securities held by him or her and the number of directors to be elected (s. 159[5][a]). A member may give all his or her votes to a single candidate or divide them between more than one of the candidates (159[5][b]). The candidate with the highest number of votes shall be declared elected first, then the candidate with the second-highest number of votes, and so on until the total number of directors to be elected has been so chosen (s. 159[5][c]). Thus, the act provides for a system of cumulative voting, which ensures a better representation of minority interests than election by simple plurality or majority of votes.

Regarding the removal of directors, s. 163(1) provides that a director can be removed with or without cause by the company by resolution in general meeting. In order to preserve minority representation in accordance with the system of cumulative voting, such resolution shall not be deemed to have been passed if the number of votes cast against it is equal to, or exceeds:

- Total number of votes for the time being computed in the manner laid down in s. 159(5)(a) divided by the number of directors for the time being, if the resolution relates to removal of a director appointed under s. 157 (first directors of the company), s. 161 (director appointed by other director due to casual vacancy), and s. 162 (fresh election after a member's having acquired the requisite shareholding to be elected as a director).

- Minimum number of votes that were cast for the election of a director at the immediately preceding election of directors, if the resolution relates to removal of a director elected in the manner provided in s. 159.

### Directors' Duties

Until the reforms of 2017, directors' duties were not codified in Pakistan. They are now laid down in s. 204 of the Companies Act, 2017. According to this provision, the duties of directors include:

- acting in accordance with the articles of association;
- acting in good faith, promoting the object and the best interests of the company, its employees, shareholders, community, and environment;
- acting with reasonable care, skill, and diligence;
- not being involved in a situation in which the directors may have a direct or indirect interest that conflicts, or possibly may conflict, with the interest of the company;
- not achieving or attempting to achieve any undue gain or advantage for himself or herself and his or her relatives, partners, or associates; and if the director is found guilty of making any undue gain, he shall be liable to pay an amount equal to that gain to the company; and
- not assigning his office, and such assignment shall be void.

Since s. 204 is relatively new, there has only been one reported judgment interpreting what may constitute a breach of duties. In *Human Rights Case No. 3654 of 2018 (In the matter regarding appointment of Managing Director, Pakistan Television Corporation)*, the Supreme Court of Pakistan held that the concerned managing director had violated his duties under s. 204, specifically subsections 2, 3, 4, and 5 (corresponding to the second to the fifth abovementioned provision), because he:

- had hosted a show on air while he was the managing director of the television channel;
- had hired his own son as a script writer for a television drama of the channel;
- had used two instead of one official car;
- had used the channel's funds to pay his membership and subscription fees for a country club;
- had used the channel's funds to entertain his guests inside and outside of his office; and
- had used the channel's funds to attend a book exhibition completely unrelated to his duties.

It should be noted that the channel in question in this case (Pakistan Television Corporation) is a public company, i.e. a state-owned enterprise.

### Related-Party Transactions

Related-party transactions are regulated in sections 205–209 Companies Act, 2017. The regulatory regime is centered around disclosure and abstention by the interested director. Pursuant to s. 205, every director who is directly or indirectly interested in a transaction with the company must disclose the nature of his or her interest at a meeting of the board of directors as soon as possible. In a decision of the board on the interested transaction, the conflicted director is required to abstain from discussing and voting on the transaction. In the case of a listed company, the requirements are heightened.

A director who has a material personal interest in a matter that is being considered at a board meeting must not be present while that matter is being considered (s. 207[1]).

The Companies Act further requires that companies adopt a policy for dealing with related-party transactions and the general meeting approve such transactions by special resolution if a majority of the directors are conflicted (s. 208[1]). Related parties include the director, his or her relatives, managerial personnel and their relatives, and legal entities in which directors or managers are interested, but not substantial shareholders (unless the shareholder has a controlling interest in the company). The above requirements do not apply to transactions that are entered into by the company in its ordinary course of business and on an arm's length basis (s. 208[1]). Related-party transactions must be disclosed in a report to the shareholders together with a justification for entering into the transaction (s. 208[2]).

The 2019 Code also requires that the details of all related-party transactions are placed periodically before the audit committee, which gives recommendations, and presented to the board or, if a majority of directors are interested in the transaction, the general meeting for review and approval (reg. 15). However, it should be noted that this provision does not belong to the mandatory rules of the 2019 Code.

### Minority Shareholder Lawsuits

Pakistan company law does not provide for a derivative action mechanism. The two existing substitute mechanisms, both incorporated from English law, are a petition for relief because of unfairly prejudicial conduct (s. 286 Companies Act, 2017) and, closely related in its prerequisites, a petition for the winding up of the company (s. 301[g][iii] Companies Act).

Pursuant to s. 286, any member or members holding not less than 10% of the issued share capital can file a petition arguing that the affairs of the company are being conducted in an unlawful or fraudulent manner, or in a manner not provided for in its memorandum, or in a manner oppressive to any of the members or unfairly prejudicial to the public interest. The court may then make such order as it thinks fit, for example, order a change in the management of the company or the buyout of the complaining minority shareholder.

Similarly, under s. 301(g)(iii), minority shareholders may apply to court for a winding up of the company if the company is conducting its business in a manner oppressive to the minority members or persons concerned with the formation or promotion of the company. Again, in order to be eligible to file a petition, the applicants must hold not less than 10& of the equity share capital of the company. Even if they cross this threshold, it is difficult to succeed on an s. 301 or an s. 286 petition, since the onus to prove that the challenged conduct was oppressive is on the minority shareholders, and mere disappointment due to the decisions of the majority shareholders does not amount to oppression.[7]

An example of unfairly prejudicial behavior toward the minority from the case law is the complete failure to maintain and keep books of account including trial balances, accounting ledgers, cash book, bank book, bank statements, fixed assets register, member register, minutes book, and other relevant statutory corporate and accounting records and documents.[8]

---

[7]    Muhammad Kamran Nadeem and 11 others vs. Webcom (Pvt.) Ltd. through Chief Executive (2016 CLD 1277).
[8]    In the matter of Progressive Insurance Company Ltd. (2009 CLD 1602).

## *Sri Lanka*

### Overview of the Regulatory Framework

Companies are governed by the Companies Act 2007. In addition, Sri Lanka's Institute of Chartered Accountants and the Securities and Exchange Commission of Sri Lanka have issued a Code of Best Practice on Corporate Governance that has been updated regularly since 1997, most recently in 2017. The corporate governance standards were incorporated into the listing rules of the Colombo Stock Exchange (CSE) in 2007 (Listing Rules, section 7.10) and, accordingly, have become mandatory for listed companies. More recent editions of the corporate governance code in 2008, 2013, and 2017 establish voluntary best practice standards. The listing rules have been amended since their adoption, but they are not identical to the voluntary code, and not all recent changes in the voluntary code have been carried over to the listing rules.

### Board Structure

Table 6 gives an overview of the regulation of corporate boards in Sri Lanka along the five dimensions that section 1.2 identified as critical in ensuring that boards operate as an effective, independent control mechanism, as well as the manner in which the regulatory requirements are enforced. The requirements of both the Code of Best Practice on Corporate Governance 2017 and the CSE Listing Rules 2007 are reported.

## Table 6: Board Structure Regulation in Sri Lanka

| Dimension | Regulatory Requirements Applicable to Listed Companies | Summary |
|---|---|---|
| Proportion of nonexecutive directors | **Corporate Governance Code 2017, A.5:** It is preferable for the board to have a balance of executive and nonexecutive directors such that no individual or small group of individuals can dominate the board's decision-taking.<br>**A.5.1:** The board should include nonexecutive directors of sufficient caliber and number for their views to carry significant weight in the board's decisions. The board should include at least three nonexecutive directors or such number of nonexecutive directors equivalent to one-third of the total number of directors, whichever is higher. In the event the chair and chief executive officer (CEO) is the same person, or if the chairman is not an independent director, nonexecutive directors should comprise a majority of the board.<br>**Listing Rules, s. 7.10.1:** The board of directors of a Listed Entity shall include at least two nonexecutive directors or such number of nonexecutive directors equivalent to one-third of the total number of directors, whichever is higher. | One-third |
| Number of independent directors | **Corporate Governance Code 2017, A.5.2:** Where the constitution of the board of directors includes only three nonexecutive directors, all three nonexecutive directors should be independent. In all other instances, all three or two nonexecutive directors appointed to the board of directors, whichever is higher, should be independent.<br>**Listing Rules, s. 7.10.2:** Where the constitution of the board of directors includes only two nonexecutive directors, both nonexecutive directors shall be independent. In all other instances, two or one nonexecutive director appointed to the board of directors, whichever is higher, shall be independent. | Three directors or two-thirds of nonexecutive directors |
| Definition of independence | **Corporate Governance Code 2017, A.5.3:** For a director to be deemed independent, such director should be independent of management and free of any business or other relationship that could materially interfere with or could reasonably be perceived to materially interfere with the exercise of their unfettered and independent judgment.<br>**A.5.5:** A director would not be independent if he or she: has been employed by the company, subsidiary, or parent of the company during the period of 2 years immediately preceding appointment;<br>• currently has or has had, within the last 2 years immediately preceding appointment as director, a material business relationship with the company, whether directly or indirectly;<br>• has or has had in the preceding financial year, a close family member who is a director or CEO, or key management personnel;<br>• is a significant shareholder of the company or an officer of, or otherwise associated directly with, a significant shareholder of the company;<br>• has served on the board of the company continuously for a period exceeding 9 years from the date of the first appointment;<br>• is employed in another company or business:<br>  – in which a majority of the other directors of the company are employed or are directors; or<br>  – in which a majority of the other directors of the company have a significant shareholding or material business relationship; or<br>  – that has a significant shareholding in the company or with which the company has a business connection;<br>• is a director of another company:<br>  – in which a majority of the other directors of the company are employed or are directors; or<br>  – that has a business connection with the company or significant shareholding in the company; and<br>• has a material business relationship or a significant shareholding in another company or business:<br>  – in which a majority of the other directors of the company are employed or are directors; and/or<br>  – which has a business connection with the company or significant shareholding in the same.<br>The capitalized terms are further defined in the Corporate Governance Code.<br>**Listing Rules, s. 7.10.4,** imposes similar independence criteria. | Detailed and demanding definition |

continued on next page

*Table 6 continued*

| Dimension | Regulatory Requirements Applicable to Listed Companies | Summary |
|---|---|---|
| Separation of chair and CEO | **Corporate Governance Code 2017, A.2:** There should be a clear division of responsibilities at the head of the company, which will ensure a balance of power and authority, such that no one individual has unfettered powers of decision. **A.2.1:** A decision to combine the posts of chair and CEO in one person should be justified and highlighted in the annual report. **A.5.7:** In the event the chairman and CEO is the same person, the board should appoint one of the independent nonexecutive directors to be the senior independent director and disclose this appointment in the annual report. **Listing Rules, s. 7.10.1:** not required | Not strictly required but encouraged |
| Committee structure | **Succession planning** **Corporate Governance Code 2017, A.7.1:** A Nomination Committee should be established to make recommendations to the board on all new board appointments. **Schedule A:** Majority of the Membership of the Committee shall be nonexecutive directors and shall include at least one or one-third (whichever is higher) of independent nonexecutive directors. The chair of the committee shall be an independent nonexecutive director appointed by the board. **Listing Rules, s. 7.10.1:** not required **Audit** **Corporate Governance Code 2017, D.3.1:** The board should establish an audit committee exclusively of nonexecutive directors with a minimum of three nonexecutive directors, of whom at least two should be independent. If there are more nonexecutive directors, the majority should be independent. The committee should be chaired by an independent nonexecutive director. The board should satisfy itself that at least one member of the audit committee has recent and relevant experience in financial reporting and control. **Listing Rules, s. 7.10.6:** A Listed Entity shall have an audit committee that shall comprise of a minimum of two independent nonexecutive directors (in instances where the entity has only two directors on its board) or of nonexecutive directors a majority of whom shall be independent, whichever shall be higher. The chair or one member of the committee should be a member of a recognized professional accounting body. **Remuneration** **Corporate Governance Code 2017, B.1.1:** To avoid potential conflicts of interest, the board of directors should set up a Remuneration Committee to make recommendations to the board on the company's framework of remunerating executive directors. **B.1.2:** Remuneration committees should consist exclusively of nonexecutive directors with a minimum of three nonexecutive directors of whom the majority should be independent. The chair should be an independent nonexecutive director and should be appointed by the board. **Listing Rules, s. 7.10.5:** A Listed Entity shall have a remuneration committee that shall comprise of a minimum of two independent nonexecutive directors (in instances where the entity has only two directors on its board) or of nonexecutive directors, a majority of whom shall be independent, whichever shall be higher. | Nomination: yes Audit: yes Remuneration: yes |
| Enforcement | **Corporate Governance Code 2017:** voluntary **Listing Rules:** mandatory | Largely mandatory |

Source: Authors.

## Further Minority Protection Mechanisms

### Appointment and Removal of Directors

Pursuant to s. 204(2) Companies Act 2007, all directors are appointed by ordinary resolution, unless the articles of the company provide otherwise. Directors must be voted on individually, unless the general meeting resolves unanimously to allow the appointment of two or more persons as directors by a single resolution (s. 205). Subject to the articles, directors may be removed from office at any time by ordinary resolution with or without cause (s. 206[1]).

### Directors' Duties

Sections 187–190 of the Companies Act 2007 set out the duties of directors. According to these provisions, directors are subject to the following three main duties:

- Directors must act in good faith in what they believe to be in the interests of the company (s. 187).
- Directors must not act in a manner that contravenes any requirements of the Companies Act or the articles of association (s. 188).
- Pursuant to s. 189, a person exercising powers or performing duties as a director:
  - shall not act in a manner which is reckless or grossly negligent; and
  - shall exercise the degree of skill and care that may reasonably be expected of a person of his knowledge and experience.

### Related-Party Transactions

Related-party transactions are regulated in sections 191–197 Companies Act 2007. A director who is directly or indirectly materially interested in a transaction with the company must disclose the nature and extent of the interest to the board of directors, and cause it to be entered in an "interests register' that has to be maintained by the company (s. 192[1]). Examples of indirect interests include material financial benefit in another entity that is a party to the transaction; being a director, officer, or trustee of another party to the transaction (unless this other party is the company's holding company or a wholly owned subsidiary); or being the parent, child, or spouse of the person who transacts with the company (s. 191[1]).

Apart from the above disclosure obligation, the approach under the Companies Act 2007 is characterized by contractual freedom. The founders of the company can determine in the articles of association whether the interested director can attend the board meeting at which the transaction is discussed, be counted for purpose of a quorum at that meeting, and indeed vote on the related-party transaction. If no provision to the contrary is contained in the articles, an interested director may perform all of these actions (s. 196).

Section 9 of the CSE Listing Rules impose additional, binding requirements on listed companies, including shareholder approval by special resolution if the transaction passes certain asset or revenue thresholds.

*Minority Shareholder Lawsuits*

Minority shareholders have two avenues to pursue claims for wrongdoing other than those encroaching upon a personal right (in which case they could bring an individual claim in their own name). Pursuant to sections 224–226 Companies Act 2007, shareholders constituting not less than 5% of the total number of shareholders, or whose shares carry not less than 5% of the voting rights in the company, may bring a complaint alleging that the affairs of the company are being conducted in a manner oppressive to the shareholders or prejudicial to the interests of the company.

The Companies Act 2007 also provides for a derivative action mechanism, which is laid down in sections 234–237. Under this route, any shareholder or director of a company may apply to the court to bring proceedings in the name and on behalf of the company. In determining whether to grant leave to continue the proceedings, the court will consider the likelihood of the litigation succeeding, the costs of the litigation in relation to the relief likely to be obtained, the interests of the company in the proceedings being commenced, and whether it is in the interests of the company that the conduct of the proceedings should not be left to the directors or to the determination of the shareholders as a whole (s. 234). If leave is granted under these provisions, the court may order that the reasonable costs of bringing the litigation shall be met by the company (s. 235).

# Conclusion

Corporate governance frameworks in South Asia have undergone a process of comprehensive modernization over recent years. In all member countries of the South Asian Association for Regional Cooperation (SAARC), except Afghanistan, Bhutan, and Nepal, corporate governance codes have been adopted. The codes surveyed for this study are generally comparable to internationally accepted standards of best practice in corporate governance (although they do, in certain aspects, fall short of these benchmarks[9]). In order to illustrate where the codes in force in South Asia (and Nepal's Companies Act) conform to, or diverge from, international best practice standards, we use the most recent United Kingdom (UK) Corporate Governance Code (adopted in 2018) as a benchmark. The UK is generally regarded as being at the forefront of developments in corporate governance since it promulgated the world's first corporate governance code in 1992.[10] The UK Corporate Governance Code is updated regularly, usually every 2 years, and its best practice standards have influenced standard setters worldwide. Indeed, in the South Asian countries surveyed here, concepts pioneered by UK codes, for example, the independent director and the definition of independence, have, by and large, been adopted faithfully.

---

[9] In some cases, for example, Nepal, the reason is partly that corporate governance standards are implemented in the binding company legislation.

[10] Cadbury Report: The Financial Aspects of Corporate Governance (1992).

### Table 7: Board Structure Regulation in South Asia versus the United Kingdom

| Dimension | UK | Bangladesh | Nepal | Pakistan | Sri Lanka |
|---|---|---|---|---|---|
| Proportion of nonexecutive directors | At least half of the board, excluding the chair | No minimum proportion | No minimum proportion | One-third | One-third |
| Number of independent directors | At least half of the board, excluding the chair (who should also be an independent nonexecutive director) | One-fifth | One or two | One-third | Three directors or two-thirds of nonexecutive directors |
| Definition of independence | Detailed and demanding definition | Detailed and demanding definition | Detailed and demanding definition | Detailed and demanding definition | Detailed and demanding definition |
| Separation of chair and CEO | Required | Required | Required | Required | Not strictly required but encouraged |
| Committee structure | Nomination: yes Audit: yes Remuneration: yes | Nomination: yes Audit: yes Remuneration: yes | Nomination: no Audit: yes Remuneration: no | Nomination: yes (nonmandatory) Audit: yes (mandatory) Remuneration: yes (nonmandatory) | Nomination: yes Audit: yes Remuneration: yes |
| Enforcement | Comply-or-explain | Compliance mandatory | Compliance mandatory | Largely mandatory | Largely mandatory |

Source: Authors.

Table 7 shows that the most important features of the UK Corporate Governance Code—which were successively strengthened since they were first proposed by the Cadbury Committee in 1992—have been disseminated widely and can be found in all SAARC member countries included in this study. Notably, all countries require an independent, nonexecutive element on the board, and define independence in considerable detail and in a demanding manner. All countries also require, or at least encourage, a division of responsibilities at the helm of the company in the form of a separation of the roles of CEO and chair of the board. Further, important and particularly sensitive matters prone to conflicts of interest are generally required to be delegated to board committees, which are typically required to be composed exclusively or predominantly of nonexecutive directors. The difference with the UK code, therefore, is less of a qualitative and more of a quantitative nature. Importantly, the UK Corporate Governance Code 2018 goes further than any SAARC code in providing that a majority of the board (half of all board positions plus the chair) should be composed of independent directors. Independence, in this context, includes independence from both the management and major shareholders (the latter being understood as shareholders holding 10% or more of the voting capital). This is, in this report's view, a critical requirement and the main shortcoming of current frameworks, since conflicts of interest can only be addressed effectively if the board is in a position to take action against the votes of the corporate insiders.

On the other hand, SAARC member states go further than the UK policy maker in devising most corporate governance rules as binding requirements, rather than following a comply-or-explain approach. This is commendable, since comply-or-explain relies on the existence of a liquid capital market, where issuers are willing to furnish the market with detailed corporate governance disclosures and meaningful explanations if they do not comply with a best practice standard, and investors are able to price corporate governance arrangements accurately. However, a mandatory solution also comes with certain institutional preconditions. In particular, market regulators must be sufficiently well resourced, have the necessary expertise, and be free of political influence or the influence of financially powerful market participants.

This report suggests that any future reform efforts should focus on the following two issues:

(i) **Strengthening the independence of corporate boards** by bringing provisions on the number of independent nonexecutive directors and, where necessary, the definition of independence in line with international best practice standards. More concretely, a majority of directors, including the chair, should be independent nonexecutive directors, and independence should mean that a director is independent from both the management and major (not only majority) shareholders.

(ii) **Enhancing institutional capacity** and independence by ensuring that regulators are well resourced, the sanctioning regime is appropriate, and employees are well trained and appropriately incentivized to enforce regulatory requirements without bias.

Turning to binding corporate law, the applicable rules in the surveyed countries suffer without exception from two major shortcomings. First, related-party transactions are not effectively regulated, and second, private enforcement of company law is close to non-existent. In SAARC member states, these two areas are heavily influenced by 19th and early 20th century English law, without, however, having adopted more recent reforms of the English rules that mostly address their defects.

As far as related-party transactions are concerned, the countries surveyed here require an interested director to disclose his or her interest to the board and abstain from voting on the transaction. This solution, which relies exclusively on the board to monitor related-party transactions and approve only those transactions that are in the best interest of the company, requires that the board is constituted as an independent, knowledgeable control organ. As discussed, current boards in SAARC member states are typically insider-dominated, which calls into question whether they possess the necessary independence to perform their control function effectively. A solution would be the requirement to obtain shareholder approval if an interested transaction crosses a certain asset or revenue threshold (as is currently the case in some SAARC member states, for example, in Sri Lanka pursuant to Section 9 of the CSE Listing Rules). However, such a requirement would need to be calibrated carefully, notably by ensuring that the general meeting receives sufficient information of all relevant transactions (rather than, for example, only transactions that the corporate insiders deem not to have been concluded on "arm's length" terms), and only disinterested shareholders are eligible to vote on the transaction.

As far as private enforcement is concerned, many SAARC member states rely on the concept of "unfair prejudice" or "oppression of the minority" stemming from English company law. However, the two terms are badly defined, thus generating considerable legal uncertainty, and the common understanding seems to be that they do not capture all instances of corporate misconduct or breach of directors' duties. In addition, shareholders only have standing to bring a petition if they cross a threshold that is in most cases set from 5% to 10% of the issued shares. These features make the unfair prejudice petition wholly unsuitable as a mechanism to ensure the enforcement of company law by minority shareholders where the majority engages in misconduct, and cases are accordingly extremely rare in practice. The only countries that contain a derivative action mechanism, i.e., a procedural mechanism allowing minority shareholders to enforce a claim of the company where the organ normally authorized to bring a lawsuit on behalf of the company (generally the board of directors) does not act, are Nepal and Sri Lanka. The Nepalese minority shareholder lawsuit also imposes a minimum shareholding requirement to protect against strike suits,[11] and thus does not protect small minority shareholders well. In Sri Lanka, in contrast, any shareholder may apply to the court to bring a lawsuit on behalf of the company. The court then determines whether to grant leave to continue the proceedings by considering a number of factors, including the likelihood of the litigation succeeding, the costs of the litigation, and the interests of the company in the proceedings being commenced. Thus, pursuant to this approach, the court performs the function of screening applications and distinguishing meritorious from frivolous lawsuits.

In conclusion, we also recommend:

(i) **Reforming the rules governing related-party transactions**, most importantly, by ensuring that a truly independent, well-informed organ is responsible for vetting, and deciding on, such transactions. This organ may be an appropriately constituted board of directors or, for transactions exceeding a certain threshold, the disinterested shareholders (i.e., where a majority shareholder is an interested party, approval would need to be given by a "majority of the minority").

(ii) **Adopting a modern derivative action mechanism** that facilitates access to justice by allowing any shareholder holding one share or more to bring an action, with the reasonable costs of the proceedings to be borne by the company, while providing for appropriate safeguards against strike suits (for example, by allowing the court to refuse to grant leave to continue the action if it is clearly frivolous and not in the best interest of the company).

# Bibliography

Business Roundtable. 1978. The Role and Composition of the Board of Directors of the Large Publicly Owned Corporation, 33 *Business Lawyer* 2083.

World Bank. 2017. *Doing Business 2017: Equal Opportunity for All*. Washington, DC: World Bank.

World Bank. 2019. *Doing Business 2019: Training for Reform*. Washington, DC: World Bank.

Cambridge Centre for Business Research. 2009. *Law, Finance & Development* (description and research output available at http://www.cbr.cam.ac.uk/research/research-projects/completed-projects/law-finance-development).

Cambridge Centre for Business Research. 2016. *Law, Development & Finance in Rising Powers* (description and research output available at http://www.cbr.cam.ac.uk/research/research-projects/law-development-finance-in-rising-powers).

Claessens, S. and B. Yurtoglu, 2012. Corporate Governance and Development—An Update. *IFC Focus* 10.

Gerner-Beuerle, C. 2017. Diffusion of Regulatory Innovations: The Case of Corporate Governance Codes, 13 *Journal of Institutional Economics* 271.

---

[11]    A strike suit is a lawsuit that is brought mainly to obtain a settlement, rather than because it has merit.

# 2 BOARD STRUCTURE, BOARD INDEPENDENCE, AND BOARD DIVERSITY

## Introduction

In order for a corporate governance system to work effectively, the structure and composition of the board of directors is of central importance as it is the highest decision-making body, with owners and society entrusting it to manage the firm well, and on their behalf.

But what is corporate governance, and why does it matter? In the end it is "the system by which companies are directed and controlled," as defined by the Cadbury report from 1992. It means setting the direction in which the company is going, its goals and objectives, as well as controlling the implementation of these goals with the aim to maximize the (long-term) value of firms, and to reduce its inherent risk. Typically, it is the equity investors that are most concerned about the governance systems in the firms they invest in, but it also applies to bond market investors as good governance systems will help to reduce the default risk.

Corporate governance is more than just boards, but boards being the most important day-to-day mechanism. Other mechanisms are owners (type and structure), incentive structures, company laws, and other mechanisms. Corporate governance has to be seen not as one optimal system that can be implemented in the same way globally, but as a combination of mechanisms that vary from country to country, industry to industry, and firm to firm. Corporate governance is relevant to all firms along the ownership spectrum, from widely held publicly listed companies all the way to state-owned enterprises (SOEs) with a strong controlling owner.

The board's function is to oversee, to guide the firm's central parameters of strategy and risk, be involved in CEO and other key appointments, and to "provide a sparring partner" for management, among others. Given its centrality to the functioning of the firm, societies have invested considerable resources in thinking about optimal board structures, board independence, and other criteria like board diversity that can help ensure outstanding firm performance.

The structure of this paper will be defined by these parameters. It opens with a general discussion about the importance of boards, their main goals, and how they are practically delivering these goals. The role of the chairperson will receive special attention, as the chair is ultimately responsible for the functioning of the board, setting the tone from the top, and the quality of the debate on strategic and operational issues around the board table.

Much of governance-related discussion and policy making has focused on board independence, which also feature prominently in this paper. The idea is to structure the board in a way that the majority of board members are independent of management and do not favor controlling shareholders, and so bring the necessary objectivity to decision-making and outside counsel to the firm. Independent board members were an oddity 30 years ago, but are now ubiquitous in Asia, the Americas, and Europe (Puchniak et al. 2017).[12] In his report's view, it is fair to argue the importance of the independent director to the success of corporate boards, and hence to the firm.

# On Boards

But what are boards? Formally, boards are intermediaries between shareholders and managers. They are elected by shareholders (and in some countries also by other constituencies) and must make key decisions. This includes evaluating company performance, hiring and firing company managers, formulating business strategy, and deciding on a number of issues in which managers have a special interest, such as auditing, compensation, or nomination of new board members (Thomsen et al., 2019). Often, national laws specify the minimum number of directors, and other structural requirements, which we will discuss in the respective country sections.

Most board members in both listed and non-listed firms are now part-time, nonexecutive directors who do not work for the company and only appear for board meetings and special occasions, such as the annual shareholder meeting. This was not always so and is still not the case in Japan, where most board members are still executives. In any case, in most but not all systems/countries it is customary for the CEO and other managers to sit on the board. In some countries (e.g., the United States [US], France), the chief executive can also be chairperson of the board (duality), but this is prohibited in some one-tier and most two-tier systems (which will be discussed extensively), which is common to most countries in continental Europe. In the UK, the two positions of chair and CEO are typically separated in line with the national corporate governance recommendations (Cadbury, 1992).

Countries are often grouped together into those that have one-tier, and those with two-tier boards. Some countries allow firms to choose. One-tier boards are synonymous with the US and UK, and the Anglo-American legal world more generally. In a one-tier system, the management (albeit often just the CEO and one more executive) meet together with the nonexecutives, while in a two-tier system, the management and the supervisory board meet separately. In some two-tier systems, labor representatives also join the board. This includes Germany, which gives ample voice to labor representatives, but is also a country with very modest and rationally acting unions.[13]

Boards tend to meet from six to 10 times per year, and occasionally more often than that, especially in the financial industry and in very large firms. A typical board meeting lasts from 3–4 hours to a whole day, but rarely goes beyond that. Most board members have little stock in the companies they serve. Outside the US, most nonexecutive directors are paid a fixed fee. The UK governance code and other codes advise against stock options for nonexecutives; in the US, it is the opposite.

Board members make collective decisions, as typically they represent not the interests of one shareholder but of the firm in question. In most cases, decisions are unanimous.

---

[12]    For Asia, this is clearly a step in the right direction, but it should be considered that controlling shareholders often still yield considerable power across the region.

[13]    The German example is something of a historic anomaly, as the extensive power and involvement of "labor" goes back to the post-war period where the role of the unions was central in the successful reconstruction and capital re-accumulation of what was then West Germany.

## Chairperson

The chairperson (or chair) has a special role on the board. It is the chair's role to run the board, while the CEO runs the company. Ultimately, and if things go wrong the "buck will stop" with the chair and will need to be ready to take over in times of crisis. In any case, one of the key functions of the chairperson is to establish the right tone and procedure at the top. At least in the UK, there is a clear role separation between CEO and chair, and the various chair interviewed for a previous publication (Owen and Kirchmaier, 2009) were very much in favor of this arrangement. Most of them also do not support that a CEO should move up to become chair when his time as CEO is up, as it robs the firm its opportunity to "renew" itself in terms of strategy and people. This also does not support an independent and outsider view needed by the company.

---

### Box: Role of a Chairperson

Where the posts of chairperson (or chair) and chief executive are separated, as is the case in most British companies, the effectiveness of the board depends crucially on the relationship between these two individuals and on how the chair balances that relationship with his or her relationship with outside directors. According to the familiar shorthand definition, the chair manages the board and the chief executive runs the business. But this calls for answers to a number of questions. For example, to what extent does the chair participate in the meetings that the chief executive has with senior colleagues (usually called the executive committee) that prepare submissions to the board? And if the chair does participate, and agrees with the decisions reached, how can he or she take an independent view when the proposal reaches the board? The chair deals with this issue in different ways, and there is no clear evidence that one approach is better than others. What emerges most strongly from interviews conducted for this report is the need for clarity in the chair's job description and for the chair to abide by what has been agreed. Several interviewees emphasized the importance of written job descriptions agreed with the chief executive and approved by the board. Most interviewees took the view that the chair should not involve himself or herself directly in operational decisions, but that he or she should be given every opportunity to influence them before they are taken. "Once the decision is taken, I'll support it even if I have disagreed with it," said one chair. If the chair goes beyond influencing to interfering, there will almost certainly be a breakdown of the relationship with the chief executive.

It follows that that the chair must have full confidence in the chief executive and vice versa. "It is a binary relationship. You either have total faith in your chief executive or you don't, in which case he has to quit–there is no middle way," said one interviewee. Another spoke of the "twinning" of the chair and chief executive. "I reserve the right to fire you, but I can assure you that, if I lose confidence in you, you will be the first to know." Having faith means, among other things, not getting in the chair's way. "My job is to make the chief executive a hero and not to try to grab the glory for myself," remarked another chair. While there were exceptions among the chair interviewed, the majority view was that only the chief executive should talk to the press—it was the chief executive, not the chair, who had the primary responsibility for presenting the image of the company and explaining its strategy. "I never give interviews and I never speak to investors except at the AGM (annual general meeting)," said one chairman.

Some interviewees described the relationship as paternal rather than fraternal. In an Asian context, however, the situation might be different as the chair is likely to represent the controlling shareholder, family, or state in the case of a state-owned enterprise. The issue that this might even complicate things, as the chairman can neither be perceived as being too consensual and reluctant to intervene, nor be seen as taking over the role of the executive officer. Striking a balance between these two extremes is a difficult task for any new chair in the best of times—especially, perhaps, when the company concerned is performing satisfactorily but not brilliantly, and there are faint but not yet serious doubts about the direction of the business.

Source: Authors.

---

## Board Independence

As discussed above, board independence is in all likelihood one of the most discussed topics in corporate governance. The idea is to structure the board in a way that the majority of board members are independent from management, and so bring the necessary objectivity to decision-making and outside counsel to the firm. Board independence is now a widely accepted concept both across countries and across all ownership classes. In an Asian context, the implementation of the concept varies considerably in nature across the various jurisdictions, and might often be structured to follow the text and not necessarily spirit.

Theoretically it is a very convincing concept, as it helps to solve the inherent agency conflict in boards. Agents cannot monitor themselves, nor can other agents with a vested interest be expected to do a good job. Independence is a solution. Also, independence is important to mitigate behavioral biases. Empirically, there is considerable evidence that independence is good for the firm, and firm value.[14]

What defines independence, at least formally? The UK governance code defines dependence, as that is easier to define then independence. According to that code, a director is dependent if he or she:

- has been an employee of the company or group within the last 5 years;
- has, or has had within the last 3 years, a material business relationship with the company either directly, or as a partner, shareholder, director, or senior employee of a body that has such a relationship with the company;
- has received or receives additional remuneration from the company apart from a director's fee;
- participates in the company's share option or a performance-related pay scheme, or is a member of the company's pension scheme;
- has close family ties with any of the company's advisers, directors, or senior employees;
- holds cross-directorships or has significant links with other directors through involvement in other companies or bodies;
- represents a significant shareholder; or
- has served on the board for more than 9 years from the date of their first election.

There is always a risk that corporate governance deteriorates into a box-ticking exercise. Hence, rules need to be implemented with common sense, and in the spirit of the rule or recommendation. There is always an exception to a rule, and one should not forget that the primary purpose of independence is to free board members from interference, and from being too close to management in order to give open and frank advice and vote accordingly.

The literature is full of examples where board members are formally independent according to the definition, but in reality still highly dependent on management. This is obviously counterproductive. But there are also examples of the other way around. For example, in family-owned firms, siblings might be able to provide a more honest assessment and influence each other's course of action (as members of management) than an outsider.

---

[14] To read more about the empirical evidence on independent boards, see the work of Ron Masulis, who is based at the University of New South Wales in Sydney, Australia.

Moreover, there are other important aspects of board structure which may be negatively associated with board independence. For example, many of the most competent board members may have previous affiliation with the company or its owners. Competence and motivation might at times be more important than independence. The value of independence may also depend on the firm and its situation (Duchin, Matsuyama, and Obs, 2010).

## Independent Directors in Asia

The concept of an independent director is now ubiquitous in Asia, and many Asian economies have surpassed the independence levels observed in the US or Europe, at least formally. Independent director is a widely followed concept in Asia, in general, with some notable exceptions like Japan or Taipei,China. But as discussed above, the nominal implementation of levels and/or fractions does not necessarily follow the spirit of the independent director concept.

But again in this case, while at first instance the label of independent director is common to most boards, they may be different from what Americans or British would consider independence, and also vary considerably across Asia. In fact, Puchniak (2017) calls the independent directors in Asia "decisively un-American, and surprisingly diverse." This diversity is not overly surprising, given the different nature of the economies, and with this the governance systems, across Asia. An important function of an independent director is the protection of minority shareholders against exploitation by the dominant shareholder, or the firm from the state in the case of SOEs. Over the last 10–20 years, there has been a long debate about protecting minority shareholders, and both the US and the European Union have introduced mandatory bid rules. This means that once a minimum threshold is crossed, the majority shareholder will need to bid for all remaining shares at a predetermined price. For an extensive discussion of this, and how at times it has been circumvented, see Grant, Kirchmaier, and Kirshner (2009).[15]

Individual country arrangements are discussed in the following country sections. It is worth noting that SOEs are particularly common across Asia, discussed extensively in Chapter 3. It is in this report's opinion that SOEs would be well served to also appoint a substantial number of independent directors; the SOE has to operate and compete like any other firm.

## Board Size

On board size, there is no clear academic consensus whether it really matters. Given that board sizes fell considerably over the past 3 decades, it might be difficult to assess its impact on performance conclusively. Conceptually, the literature on group size is followed. Initially, small groups benefit from the additional knowledge and experience each board member brings to the table. Eventually, and as the group increases in size, communication and coordination costs increase, and the net benefit of each new member decreases and eventually becomes negative. It is difficult to determine the optimal number as much depends on individual circumstances, but the examples in the literature mentioned optimal group size at 8-10 members.

---

[15]   J. Grant, T. Kirchmaier, and J.A. Kirshner. 2009. Financial tunnelling and the mandatory bid rule. *European Business Organization Law Review*, vol. 10, no. 2, pp. 233-253. https://doi.org/10.1017/S156675290900233X.

## Board Committees

Most listed companies have board committees for nomination (of new directors), auditing (the audit committee), and (executive and nonexecutive) compensation. The committees will typically be composed of nonexecutive directors since the executives should not be able to influence who can fire them, how their performance is measured, or how they are paid. Moreover, board committees can be regarded as a way to professionalize board works, which allows greater attention to specific functional areas. Reeb and Upadhyay (2010) find that committees add to firm value in larger boards with a greater ratio of independent directors, but lowers firm value in smaller insider-dominated boards. In a small board of say three members, committees do not make much sense.

The nomination, audit, and compensation committees are mandatory in many jurisdictions, but some companies also have committees for strategy, risk, corporate social responsibility, acquisitions, or other important issues. Auditing committees, for example, deal with financial reports, control systems, and selection of an auditor. Intuitively, the rationale seems to be to ensure that information provided to the board is reliable and not biased by the executives in their own favor. Remuneration (compensation) committees set the pay of the executives, in which they also have a vested interest. Lastly, the nomination committee is concerned with selecting board members and managers, so independence is intended to ensure that managers do not bias board composition in their own favor.

## Board Competence

It seems self-explanatory to appoint board members that have specialist knowledge in at least one domain that is of importance to the firm, but too often this is still ignored. Prior knowledge is often defined as having prior industry experience, financial literacy, information technology (IT) expertise, research and development qualification, and board and management experience; especially in fast-moving industries, university/educational background might be needed. It is not without surprise that there is academic evidence in support of this hypothesis; hence, the experience of board members has a positive impact on firm value.

## Board Diversity

Board diversity relates to level of female participation on corporate boards, and is calculated as the number of women on a board over board size. As Adams and Kirchmaier (2016a, 2016b) have shown, board gender diversity ratios are steadily increasing around the world, but from an extremely low level. This applies to both executive and nonexecutive director positions, albeit the levels are about double for the latter. They also find that levels are generally overestimated (i.e., worse than advertised), as studies focus on the very largest companies that typically have slightly better participation levels. Boards of banks, as well as those of other financial companies, appear to have higher female participation levels. The issue, though, is that boards in the banking and financial services industry are typically much larger, and after controlling for size, participation levels are actually lower than for nonfinancial firms.

The issue is that discrimination in most (but not all) countries starts early. Adams and Kirchmaier find that an important determinant of board participation levels (in particular, in finance and Science, Technology, Engineering, Mathematics [STEM]-related fields) is the level of women's academic background in mathematics. Hence, any policy initiative will need to work on improving the mathematics/STEM-related academic background of women. Participation levels in university are quite good, but given the lower math training for women, gender participation rates are generally dismal in STEM and Finance (STEM&F)-related topics. The next big hurdle is childbirth, which takes a major hit to women's' income. The long-run income "penalty" of the first child is substantial. A recent study listed the best country as Denmark with a still considerable minus 21%, and the UK as the worst (among those studied) with minus 44% versus women's expected income. Adams and Kirchmaier (2012) also show that even if the income penalty is accepted, what matters in becoming a future board member is that women return from childbirth to work full-time, not part-time. Firms can help by supporting women, for example, by offering child care in the crucial years after childbirth, or allowing more flexible work conditions.

There is a very good reason why companies should have a strong interest to for women to return full-time from childbirth. Studies often cite having more women as board members increases the performance of the firm—measured in various ways. But correlation is not causation, and as it turns out, better firms generally employ more women, and also present in the boardroom. Hence, the faster the firm brings back women after childbirth, the less likely it is to lose human capital, and so have better people at their disposal for particular jobs. Given that women form 50% of the human capital, losing even a fraction is not only morally wrong, but simply an unacceptable treatment of (human) capital.

Many countries react to the low participation rates of women on corporate boards by imposing gender quotas. While this is no doubt desirable as it constitutes a heavy-handed intervention, one needs to keep in mind that it does not solve the underlying problem of women dropping out of the labor market after childbirth. This can only be solved with adequate policies.

It is important to note that some countries are notably better than others in terms of women's participation rates. Much of it depends on local culture (which is difficult to change); post-Communist countries have much higher participation rates. The issue is that gender diversity levels are woefully low across SAARC countries, which is important to address. One by-product of higher diversity levels is that better gender ratios typically improve the independence ratio, having a double positive effect on the organization. To improve the diversity ratios, countries have resorted to increasingly dirigisme measures. While initially written as a guide into the governance codes, countries (and the European Union) have lately switched to implementing binding gender quotas. Quotas are not without problems, as they obviously intervene into the market mechanism. It also does not solve the problem of improving the supply of board level-ready females (for a discussion see Adams and Kirchmaier [2015, 2016]).[16]

---

[16] R. Adams and T. Kirchmaier. 2015. Barriers to Boardrooms. *European Corporate Governance Institute (ECGI) -Finance Working Paper No. 347/201*, Asian Finance Association (AsFA) 2013 Conference. 22 June. https://ssrn.com/abstract=2192918; and R. Adams and T. Kirchmaier. 2016. Women in Finance. *SWIFT Institute Working Paper, ECGI-Finance Working Paper No. 479/2016*. 1 September. https://ssrn.com/abstract=2798571.

# National Legal Frameworks on Board Independence and Diversity

The following sections briefly summarize the key points of the legal framework on board independence and diversity of Bangladesh, Nepal, Pakistan, and Sri Lanka.

## *Bangladesh*

The key governance regulation in Bangladesh is the Corporate Governance Code, 2018, and unless otherwise stated, this report cites from that code.

### Proportion of Nonexecutive to Executive Directors on the Board

The code stipulates that the board can have 5–20 members. Historically, it stipulated that there should be no more than two executives, which ensures an automatic majority of nonexecutive directors. However, this provision has now been dropped, and there are no requirements stipulated anymore. For completeness, we cite condition 1.1(viii)[17] of the Draft Corporate Governance Code from 2012.

### Number of Independent Directors

At least one-fifth of the total number of directors in the company's board shall be independent directors (see No. 1(2)(a) of the Corporate Governance Code, 2018).[18]

### Definition of Independence

According to Condition no. 1(2), "independent director" means a director:

   (i)    who either does not hold any share in the company or holds less than 1% shares of the total paid-up shares of the company;
   (ii)   who is not a sponsor of the company, or is not connected with any sponsor, director or nominated director, or shareholder of the company or any of its associates, sister concerns, subsidiaries, and parents, or holding entities who holds 1% or more shares of the total paid-up shares of the company on the basis of family relationship and his or her family members (note: controlling shareholder) also shall not hold abovementioned shares in the company: provided that spouse, son, daughter, father, mother, brother, sister, son-in-law, and daughter-in-law shall be considered as family members;

---

[17]  1.1 COMPOSITION OF BOARD: The number of the board members of the company shall not be less than 5 (five) and more than 20 (twenty): Provided that- (viii) maximum 2 (two) executives may represent as members of the board of directors who shall be treated as executive director(s), and that executive directors (ED) shall have at least Bachelor's degree: Provided that the executive director(s) shall not entitle to any remuneration for attending the meetings of the board or sub-committee of the board

[18]  1. Board of Directors.- (2) Independent Directors- All companies shall have effective representation of independent directors on their Boards, so that the Board, as a group, includes core competencies considered relevant in the context of each company; for this purpose, the companies shall comply with the following: (a) At least one-fifth (1/5) of the total number of directors in the company's Board shall be independent directors; any fraction shall be considered to the next integer or whole number for calculating number of independent director(s);

(iii) who has not been an executive of the company in immediately preceding 2 financial years;

(iv) who does not have any other relationship, whether pecuniary or otherwise, with the company or its subsidiary or associated companies;

(v) who is not a member or Trading Right Entitlement Certificate holder, director, or officer of any stock exchange;

(vi) who is not a shareholder, director excepting independent director, or officer of any member or Trading Right Entitlement Certificate holder of stock exchange or an intermediary of the capital market;

(vii) who is not a partner or an executive, or was not a partner or an executive, during the preceding 3 years of the concerned company's statutory audit firm or audit firm engaged in internal audit services, or audit firm conducting special audit or professional certifying compliance of this code;

(viii) who is not independent director in more than five listed companies;

(ix) who has not been convicted by a court of competent jurisdiction as a defaulter in payment of any loan or any advance to a bank or a nonbank financial institution; and

(x) who has not been convicted for a criminal offence involving moral turpitude.

## Separation of the Two Central Roles on the Board, Chair and CEO

The roles of the chair of the board and CEO have to be separated and held by different individuals (Condition No. 1(4)(a).[19]

## Does the board have to establish committees dealing with (i) succession planning, (ii) internal controls and the appointment/supervision of the external auditor, and (iii) executive remuneration?

Corporate Governance Code, 2018 does not provide for any committees for succession planning; however, it requires formation of committees for (i) internal controls and the appointment/supervision of the external auditor and (ii) executive remuneration.

Regarding internal controls and the appointment/supervision of the external auditor: The code provides for forming audit committees, and Condition No. 5(5)(c) of the code states that the audit committee shall monitor the internal audit and compliance process, approve the Internal Audit and Compliance Plan, and also review the Internal Audit and Compliance Report.[20] Moreover, Condition No. 5(5)(d) states that the audit committee shall oversee hiring and performance of the external auditors.[21]

Regarding executive remuneration: Condition No. 4 requires formation of a Nomination and Remuneration Committee (NRC) for ensuring good governance in the company. Condition No. 6(5) stipulates that NRC formulate criteria to determine qualifications, positive attributes,

[19] (4) Duality of chairperson of the board of directors and managing director or Chief Executive Officer. (a) The positions of the chairperson of the board and the managing director (MD) and/or Chief Executive Officer (CEO) of the company shall be filled by different individuals.

[20] 5. Audit Committee- 5. Role of Audit Committee: The Audit Committee shall: (c) monitor Internal Audit and Compliance process to ensure that it is adequately resourced, including approval of the Internal Audit and Compliance Plan and review of the Internal Audit and Compliance Report;

[21] 5. Audit Committee- 5. Role of Audit Committee: The Audit Committee shall:(d) oversee hiring and performance of external auditors.

and independence of a director, and thereby recommend a policy to the board of directors regarding the remuneration of directors and top-level executives.[22] In preparing the recommendation, the NRC is required to consider whether (i) the remuneration is reasonable to attract the directors to successfully run the company; (ii) the remuneration is to be based on performance the benchmarks of which shall be clearly defined; (iii) the remuneration of the directors and top-level executives shall have a balance between fixed and incentive pay; and (iv) shall also address the short- and long-term performance objectives taking into consideration the company's goals.

### Board Diversity

Neither the Companies Act, 1994, nor the Corporate Governance Code, 2018, contains any provision regarding gender quotas which make inclusion of women on the board mandatory. However, the code requires the NRC to devise a policy on board diversity, taking into consideration age, gender, experience, ethnicity, educational background and nationality (Condition No. 6[5][b][ii]).

## Nepal

Nepal has adopted no corporate governance code, but some requirements concerning board structure and board diversity are contained in the binding company law, the Companies Act, 2006. The following summary is based on the requirements of this act.

### Proportion of Nonexecutive to Executive Directors on the Board

The Companies Act, 2006 draws no distinction between executive and nonexecutive directors; hence, as opposed to the other countries surveyed, there is no minimum proportion of nonexecutive directors on the board. However, the act requires one or, on large boards with more than seven directors, two directors to be independent, which means that they have to be nonexecutives.[23]

### Number of Independent Directors

If the board is composed of not more than seven directors, at least one director, must be independent; if the board is composed of more than seven directors, at least two directors must be independent (s. 86[3] Companies Act, 2006).[24]

---

[22]    6. Nomination and Remuneration Committee (NRC).(5) Role of the NRC(b) NRC shall oversee, among others, the following matters and make report with recommendation to the Board: (i) formulating the criteria for determining qualifications, positive attributes and independence of a director and recommend a policy to the Board, relating to the remuneration of the directors, top level executive, considering the following: (a) the level and composition of remuneration is reasonable and sufficient to attract, retain and motivate suitable directors to run the company successfully; (b) the relationship of remuneration to performance is clear and meets appropriate performance benchmarks; and (c) remuneration to directors, top level executive involves a balance between fixed and incentive pay reflecting short and long-term performance objectives appropriate to the working of the company and its goals.

[23]    Section 86. Board of directors and number of directors: (1) The appointment and number of directors of a private company shall be as provided in its articles of association. (2) Every public company shall have a board of directors consisting of a minimum of three and a maximum of eleven directors. (3) In forming the board of directors pursuant to Sub-section (2), at least one independent director, in the case of the number of directors not exceeding seven, and at least two independent directors, in the case of the number of directors exceeding seven, shall be appointed from amongst the persons who have the knowledge as prescribed in the articles of association of the company and gained knowledge and experience in the subject related with the business of the company concerned. (4) Any one director selected by the directors from amongst themselves shall be the Chairperson of the board of directors.

[24]    See footnote 23.

## Definition of Independence

Independence is defined (negatively) by s. 89(2) Companies Act, 2006 as follows:

Any of the following persons shall not be eligible to be appointed to the office of independent director:

(i)     who is not eligible to be appointed as a director pursuant to s. 89(1);[25]
(ii)    who is a shareholder of the concerned company;
(iii)   who has not obtained at least bachelor's degree in a subject that is related to the business to be carried on by the concerned company, and gained at least 10 years of experience in the related field or in the company management affairs, or who has not obtained at least a bachelor's degree in finance, economics, management, accounts, statistics, commerce, trade, or law and gained at least 10 years of experience in the related field;
(iv)    who is an officer, auditor, or employee of the concerned company, or a period of 3 years has not lapsed after his or her retirement from any such office;
(v)     who is the close relative of the office of the concerned company; and
(vi)    who is an auditor of the concerned company or his or her partner.

## Separation of the Two Central Roles on the Board, Chair and CEO

The Listed Companies Corporate Governance Directive, 2018, issued by the Securities Board of Nepal, prohibits the position of both chair and CEO to be held by the same person. This directive is binding and has been issued as part of the securities board's powers under the Securities Act, 2006, to adopt regulations and directives concerning public companies that have securities listed on the Nepal Stock Exchange.

## Does the board have to establish committees dealing with (i) succession planning, (ii) internal controls and the appointment/supervision of external auditor, and (iii) executive remuneration?

The Companies Act, 2006 requires the establishment of an audit committee, but not of other committees concerning succession planning or remuneration. The audit committee must consist of

[25] Section 89(1) provides: Any of the following persons shall not be eligible to be appointed to the office of director: (a) Who is below Twenty one years of age, in the case of a public company; (b) Who is of unsound mind or is insane; (c) Who is a declared insolvent and a period of five years has not lapsed; (d) Who is convicted of an offense of corruption or of an offense involving moral turpitude. Provided, that in the case of a private company, a period of three years has not lapsed from the date of such sentence, (e) who is convicted of an offense of theft, fraud, forgery or embezzlement or misuse of goods or funds entrust to him/her, in an authorized manner, and sentenced in respect thereof, a period of three year has not elapsed from the expiry of the sentence; (f) who has personal interest of any kind in the business or any contract or transaction of the concerned company; (g) who is already a director, substantial shareholder, employee, auditor or adviser of another company having similar objectives or has personal interest of any kind in such company; Provided, however, that such person of a private company may become a director of another private company having similar objectives. (h) who is a shareholder that is held to have failed to pay any amount due and payable by him/her to the concerned; (i) In the case of a person who has been sentenced to punishment pursuant to Section 160, a period of one year is not lapsed from the date of sentence, or in the case of a person who has been sentenced to punishment pursuant to Section 161, a period of six months has not lapsed after the date of sentence; (j) In the event that the prevailing laws prescribed any qualification or disqualification in the case of a company carrying on any specific business, who does not possess such qualification or suffers from such disqualification; (k) Who is already a director of any company which has not submitted such reruns and reports as required to be submitted to the Office under this Act, for any continuous three financial years; (l) Who is holding the office of director receiving from another listed company any remuneration or facility, other than a meeting allowance and actual expenses to be in curried in coming to, going from, and staying in, the place of meeting.

at least three members and be chaired by a nonexecutive director. Further, at least one member of the audit committee must have financial expertise (s. 164 Companies Act, 2006).[26]

It is in this report's opinion that it would be sensible to go beyond the minimum requirements and follow international norms to establish, besides the audit committee, at least a nomination and remuneration committee.

### Board Diversity

The Nepalese Companies Act 2006 makes no provision for gender quotas on corporate boards.

## Pakistan

The main governance regulation in Pakistan is based on the Listed Companies (Code of Corporate Governance) Regulations, 2019 (hereinafter referred to as 2019 Code), and refers back to the Companies Act of 2017.

### Proportion of Nonexecutive to Executive Directors on the Board

Section 154 of the Companies Act, 2017 (hereinafter referred to as 2017 Act) states that a listed company should not have less than seven directors. Regulation 8 of the 2019 Code states that the number of executive directors should not be more than one-third of the board of directors, hence a clear majority of nonexecutive directors.[27]

---

[26]   Section 164. Audit Committee: (1) A listed capital with paid up capital of thirty million rupees or more or a company which is fully or partly owned by the Government of Nepal shall form an audit committee under the Chairpersonship of a director who is not involved in the day-to-day operations of the company and consisting of a least three members. (2) An person who is a close relative of the chief executive of a company shall not be eligible to be a member of the audit committee formed pursuant to Sub-section (1). (3) At least one member of the audit committee shall be an experienced person having obtained professional certificate on accounting or a person having gained experience in accounting and financial field after having obtained at least bachelor's degree in accounts, commerce, management, finance or economics. (4) The report of board of directors required to be prepared by a company shall set out a short description of the activities of the audit committee, working policies adopted by the board of directors to implement the suggestions, if any, given by the audit committee, the allowances or facilities ,if any, received by the members or the audit committee and the names of the members of audit committee. (5) The audit committee may, for inquiring into any matter, notify the managing director of the company, chief executive or the company or other director, auditor, internal auditor and accounts chief involved in the day-to-day operations of the company to attend its meeting; and it shall be their duty to be present in the meeting of that committee if they are so notified. (6) The board of directors shall implement the suggestions given by the audit committee in respect of the accounts and financial management the company; and where any suggestion cannot be implemented, the board of directors shall also mention the reasons for the same in its report. (7) A company shall arrange for such means and resources as may be adequate for the fulfillment of responsibilities of the audit committee; and the audit committee may fix its internal rules of procedures on its own. (8) The chairperson of the audit committee shall be present in the annual general meeting of the company.(9) The audit committee shall meet as per necessity.

[27]   Reg. 8. Executive Director.- (1) It is mandatory that the executive directors, including the chief executive officer, shall not be more than one third of the Board. (2) For the purpose of compliance with the requirement of the above sub-regulation (1), the Board shall be reconstituted not later than expiry of its current term. Explanation I.—For the purposes of this regulation, a listed company shall explain the reasons, in compliance report, any fraction contained in such one-third number which is rounded up as one. Explanation II.- Executive director means a director who devotes the whole or substantially the whole of his time (whether paid or not) to the operations of the company.

## Number of Independent Directors

Reg. 6 of the 2019 Code states that independent directors of companies should not be less than two-thirds or one-third of the total members of the board, whichever is higher.[28]

## Definition of Independence

The 2019 Code does not provide a definition of an independent director. However, the definition is provided in the Companies Act, 2017, and Reg. 2 states that words and expressions used in the 2019 Code should have the same meaning as the 2017 Act. Section 166(2) of the Companies Act, 2017, defines an independent director as "a director who is not connected or does not have any relationship, whether pecuniary or otherwise, with the company, its associated companies, subsidiaries, holding company or directors; and he can be reasonably perceived as being able to exercise independent business judgment without being subservient to any form of conflict of interest."

## Separation of the Two Central Roles on the Board, Chair and CEO

Reg. 9 of the 2019 Code states that "the Chairman and the chief executive officer of a company, by whatever name called, shall not be the same person."

## Does the board have to establish committees dealing with (i) succession planning, (ii) internal controls and the appointment/supervision of external auditor, and (iii) executive remuneration?

The 2019 Code contains provisions regarding the composition of various committees.

(i) **Committee for Succession Planning**

The 2019 Code provides for the establishment of a nomination committee in Reg. 29.[29] The nomination committee is responsible for making recommendations to the board regarding the composition of committees of the board. Succession planning (and performance evaluation) of key executive personnel, on the other hand, is overseen by the Human Resources and

---

[28]　Reg. 6. Independent Director.- (1) It is mandatory that each listed company shall have at least two or one third members of the Board, whichever is higher, as independent directors. Explanation.—For the purposes of this sub-regulation, a listed company shall explain the reasons, in the compliance report, if any fraction contained in such one-third number which is not rounded up as one. (2) For the purpose of electing independent director, the Board shall be reconstituted not later than expiry of its current term. (3) It is mandatory that the independent director shall submit his consent to act as director, along with declaration to the company that he qualifies the criteria of independence notified under the Act and such declaration shall be submitted to chairman of the Board at first meeting which is held after election of directors as well as on an event of any change affecting his independence.

[29]　Reg. 29. Nomination Committee.- (1) The Board may constitute a separate committee, designated as the nomination committee, of such number and class of directors, as it may deem appropriate in its circumstances. (2) The nomination committee shall be responsible for,- (i) considering and making recommendations to the Board in respect of the Board's committees and the chairmanship of the Board's committees; and (ii) keeping the structure, size and composition of the Board under regular review and for making recommendations to the Board with regard to any changes necessary. (3) The terms of reference of nomination committee shall be determined by the Board ensuring there is no duplication or conflict with matters stipulated under terms of reference of Human Resource and Remuneration (HR&R) Committee.

Remuneration (HR&R) Committee, to be established pursuant to Reg. 28.[30] The terms of reference of the HR&R Committee may be determined by the board of directors and this may include recommending to the board of directors the selection, evaluation, development, and compensation of chief operating officer, chief financial officer, company secretary, and head of internal audit. Further, Reg. 10(4)(b) states that the board of directors shall maintain a complete record of policies regarding human resource management including preparation of a succession plan.

(ii)  **Committee for Internal Controls and the Appointment/Supervision of External Auditor**
The 2019 Code provides for a Risk Management Committee (Reg. 30). The terms of reference of this committee, which will be determined by the board, may include:
a.  monitoring and review of all material controls (financial, operational, compliance);
b.  robust risk management measures, and ensuring integrity of financial information; and
c.  appropriate extent of disclosure of company's risk framework and internal control system in directors' report.[31]

A separate committee is also in place by virtue of Reg. 27: the Audit Committee. Pertinently, Reg. 27(4)(xv) states that the Audit Committee shall give recommendations to the board regarding the appointment of the external auditors, their removal, and other matters, and the board is compelled to give due consideration to these recommendations and if it disagrees with any of them, it shall give reasons for doing so. Reg. 27 provides that the board of directors shall determine the terms of reference of the Audit Committee and they shall include, *inter alia*, review of annual and interim financial statements prior to the approval by the board, facilitating

---

[30]  Reg. 28. Human Resource and Remuneration Committee.- (1) There shall be a human resource and remuneration committee of at least three members comprising a majority of non-executive directors of whom at least one member shall be an independent director. (2) The chairman of the committee shall be an independent director and the chief executive officer may be included as a member of the committee. (3) The committee shall meet at least once in a financial year and may meet more often if requested by a member of the Board, or committee itself or the chief executive officer and the head of human resource or any other person appointed by the Board may act as the secretary of the committee. (4) The chief executive officer (if not a member of the committee), head of human resource (if not the secretary to committee), or any other advisor or person may attend the meeting only by invitation. (5) A member of the committee shall not participate in the proceedings of the committee when an agenda item relating to his performance or review or renewal of the terms and conditions of his service comes up for consideration. (6) The terms of reference of committee shall be determined by the Board which may include the following,- (i) recommendation to the Board for consideration and approval a policy framework for determining remuneration of directors (both executive and non-executive directors and members of senior management). The definition of senior management will be determined by the Board which shall normally include the first layer of management below the chief executive officer level; (ii) undertaking, annually, a formal process of evaluation of performance of the Board as a whole and its committees either directly or by engaging external independent consultant and if so appointed, a statement to that effect shall be made in the directors' report disclosing therein name and qualifications of such consultant and major terms of his / its appointment; (iii) recommending human resource management policies to the Board; (iv) recommending to the Board the selection, evaluation, development, compensation (including retirement benefits) of chief operating officer, chief financial officer, company secretary and head of internal audit; (v) consideration and approval on recommendations of chief executive officer on such matters for key management positions who report directly to chief executive officer or chief operating officer; and (vi) where human resource and remuneration consultants are appointed, they shall disclose to the committee their credentials and as to whether they have any other connection with the company.

[31]  Reg. 30. Risk Management Committee.- (1) The Board may constitute the risk management committee, of such number and class of directors, as it may deem appropriate in its circumstances, to carry out a review of effectiveness of risk management procedures and present a report to the Board. (2) The terms of reference of the committee may include the following,- (i) monitoring and review of all material controls (financial, operational, compliance); (ii) risk mitigation measures are robust and integrity of financial information is ensured; and (iii) appropriate extent of disclosure of company's risk framework and internal control system in Directors report.

external auditors, ensuring coordination between internal and external auditors, reviewing the extent and scope of internal audit, etc.[32]

It is important to note that the 2019 Code provides separate criteria for the internal and external auditor.[33]

(iii) **Executive Remuneration**

Regarding remuneration, Reg. 16 and 17 of the 2019 Code state that the board shall have in place a policy regarding the remuneration of the directors and no director shall determine his or her own remuneration. Reg. 20 states that the board of directors shall determine the remuneration of the CEO, company secretary, and the internal auditor. Reg. 28(6)(i) allows the HR&R Committee to recommend to the board a policy framework for determining the remuneration of directors (executive and nonexecutive, and members of senior management which include everyone who is one level below the CEO).[34]

## Board Diversity

The 2019 Code provides, in Reg. 4, that it is mandatory for listed companies to have at least one woman on their board of directors.

In addition, Sec. 154 of the Companies Act, 2017, states that "public interest companies shall be required to have female representation on their board as may be specified by the Commission." Public interest companies are all listed companies and certain non-listed companies, including public sector companies (i.e., SOEs), public utilities, and financial services companies holding assets in a fiduciary capacity for a broad group of outsiders (Third Schedule to the Companies Act, 2017).

---

[32]  On the composition of the audit committee, see Reg. 27. Audit Committee.- (1) It is mandatory that the audit committee shall be constituted by the Board keeping in view the following requirements,- (i) the Board shall establish an audit committee of at least three members comprising of non-executive directors and at least one independent director; (ii) chairman of the committee shall be an independent director, who shall not be the chairman of the Board; (iii) the Board shall satisfy itself that at least one member of the audit committee shall be "financially literate";. Explanation:- for the purposes of this clause the expression, "financial literate" means a person who,- (a) is a member of a recognized body of professional accountants; or (b) has a post-graduate degree in finance from a university or equivalent institution, either in Pakistan or abroad, recognized by the Higher Education Commission of Pakistan; or (c) has at least ten (10) years of experience as audit committee member; or (d) at least twenty (20) years of senior management experience in overseeing of financial, audit related matters. (iv) the Audit Committee of a company shall appoint a secretary of the committee who shall either be the company secretary or head of internal audit.

[33]  On the internal audit, see Reg. 31. Composition of internal audit function.- (1) There shall be an internal audit function in every company. (2) The head of internal audit shall functionally report to the audit committee and administratively to the chief executive officer and his performance appraisal shall be done jointly by the Chairman of the audit committee and the chief executive officer. (3) No director on the Board, shall be appointed, in any capacity, in the internal audit function of the company. (4) The Board shall ensure that the internal audit team comprises of experts of relevant disciplines in order to cover all major heads of accounts maintained by the company. (5) The company shall ensure that head of internal audit is suitably qualified, experienced and conversant with the company's policies and procedures. (6) The internal audit function, wholly or partially, may be outsourced by the company to a professional services firm or be performed by the internal audit staff of holding company and in lieu of outsourcing, the company shall appoint or designate a fulltime employee other than chief financial officer, as head of internal audit holding equivalent qualification prescribed under these Regulations, to act as coordinator between firm providing internal audit services and the Board: Provided that while outsourcing the function, the company shall not appoint its existing external auditors or any of its associated company or associated undertaking, as internal auditors. (7) All companies shall ensure that internal audit reports are provided for the review of external auditors. (8) The auditors shall discuss any major findings in relation to the reports with the audit committee, which shall report matters of significance to the Board.

[34]  The text of Reg. 28 is reproduced in footnote 30.

### *Sri Lanka*

Sri Lanka has issued a Code of Best Practice on Corporate Governance that has been updated regularly since 1997, most recently in 2017. The corporate governance standards were incorporated into the listing rules of the Colombo Stock Exchange (CSE) in 2007 (Listing Rules, section 7.10) and, accordingly, have become mandatory for listed companies.

#### Proportion of Nonexecutive to Executive Directors on the Board

The board should include at least three nonexecutive directors or such number of nonexecutive directors equivalent to one-third of the total number of directors, whichever is higher.[35] In the event the chair and CEO is the same person, or if the chair is not an independent director, nonexecutive directors should comprise a majority of the board.[36]

#### Number of Independent Directors

Where the constitution of the board of directors includes only three nonexecutive directors, all three nonexecutive directors should be independent. In all other instances three or two-thirds of nonexecutive directors appointed to the board of directors whichever is higher should be independent.[37]

#### Definition of Independence

Independence is broadly defined as meaning independence of the management and the absence of any business or other relationship that could materially interfere with or could reasonably be perceived to materially interfere with the exercise of their unfettered and independent judgment. The Corporate Governance Code further lists a number of factors that militate against a director being qualified as independent.[38] These include:

- employment by the company, subsidiary, or parent of the company during the period of 2 years immediately preceding appointment;
- material business relationships with the company, whether directly or indirectly;
- a close family member being a director or CEO, or key management personnel of the company;
- significant shareholding in the company or being an officer of, or otherwise associated directly with, a significant shareholder of the company;
- service on the board continuously for a period exceeding 9 years from the date of the first appointment;

---

[35]   Corporate Governance Code 2017, A.5.1: The Board should include Non-Executive Directors of sufficient caliber and number for their views to carry significant weight in the Board's decisions. The Board should include at least three Non-Executive Directors or such number of Non-Executive Directors equivalent to one third of the total number of Directors, whichever is higher. In the event the Chairman and CEO is the same person, or if the Chairman is not an independent director, Non-Executive Directors should comprise a majority of the Board.

[36]   Footnote 35.

[37]   Corporate Governance Code 2017, A.5.2: Where the constitution of the Board of Directors includes only three Non-Executive Directors, all three Non-Executive Directors should be 'independent'. In all other instances three or two thirds of Non-Executive Directors appointed to the Board of Directors whichever is higher should be 'independent'.

[38]   Corporate Governance Code 2017, A.5.5.

- employment in another company or business in which a majority of the other directors of the company are employed or are directors, or have a significant shareholding or material business relationship, or that has a significant shareholding in the company; and
- being a director of another company in which a majority of the other directors are employed or are directors, or that has a business connection with the company or significant shareholding in the company.

## Separation of the Two Central Roles on the Board, Chair and CEO

The Corporate Governance Code requires a clear division of responsibilities at the head of the company, such that no one individual has unfettered powers of decision.[39] A decision to combine the posts of chair of the board and CEO in one person must be justified and highlighted in the annual report.[40] Further, in case the roles of chair and CEO are combined, the board should appoint one of the independent nonexecutive directors to be "Senior Independent Director" and disclose this appointment in the annual report.[41]

## Does the board have to establish committees dealing with (i) succession planning, (ii) internal controls and the appointment/supervision of external auditor, and (iii) executive remuneration?

The Corporate Governance Code recommends the establishment of nomination, audit, and remuneration committees. The nomination committee should be composed of a majority of nonexecutive directors and include at least one or one-third (whichever is higher) of independent nonexecutive directors.[42] The audit and remuneration committees should be composed exclusively of nonexecutive directors, a majority of whom should be independent.[43] At least one member of the audit committee must have recent and relevant experience in financial reporting and control.[44]

## Board Diversity

Neither the Sri Lankan Companies Act 2007 nor the Corporate Governance Code contains any provision regarding gender quotas. However, the Corporate Governance Code mentions in Schedule A (terms of reference for the nomination committee) that the nomination committee shall review regularly the composition of the board, including gender representation.

---

[39]  Corporate Governance Code 2017, A.2.
[40]  Corporate Governance Code 2017, A.2.1.
[41]  Corporate Governance Code 2017, A.5.7.
[42]  Corporate Governance Code 2017, A.7.1: A Nomination Committee should be established to make recommendations to the Board on all new Board appointments.
Schedule A: Majority of the Membership of the Committee shall be Non-Executive Directors and shall include at least one or one third (whichever is higher) of Independent Non-Executive Directors. The Chairman of the Committee shall be an Independent Non-Executive Director appointed by the Board.
[43]  Corporate Governance Code 2017, **B.1.1:** To avoid potential conflicts of interest, the Board of Directors should set up a Remuneration Committee to make recommendations to the Board on the Company's framework of remunerating executive directors. **B.1.2:** Remuneration Committees should consist exclusively of Non-Executive Directors with a minimum of three Non-Executive Directors of whom the majority should be independent. The Chairman should be an Independent Non-Executive Director and should be appointed by the Board. **D.3.1:** The board should establish an audit committee exclusively of non-executive directors with a minimum of three non-executive directors of whom at least two should be independent. If there are more non-executive directors, the majority should be independent. The Committee should be chaired by an independent non-executive director. The board should satisfy itself that at least one member of the audit committee has recent and relevant experience in financial reporting and control.
[44]  Corporate Governance Code 2017, D.3.1.

**Summary**

**Table 8: Summary of Key Points of the Legal Framework on Board Independence and Diversity**

| Key Point | Bangladesh | Pakistan | Nepal | Sri Lanka |
|---|---|---|---|---|
| Framework provided by | Corporate Governance Code 2018 | The Companies Act 2017 (Act) Listed Companies (Code of Corporate Governance) Regulations 2019 (Code) | The Companies Act 2006 (Act) | Code of Best Practice on Corporate Governance 2017 (Code) |
| Proportion of nonexecutive to executive directors on board | No requirement stipulated[1]. | Regulation 8 of the Code created a clear majority of nonexecutive directors by requiring executive directors to be not more than one-third of the total number of directors; the minimum number of directors for a listed company is seven (Section 154 of the Act). | No express distinction made between executive and nonexecutive members. | A.5.1 of the Code requires that the board of directors (BOD) have three nonexecutive directors, or one-third of the total members of the BOD must be nonexecutive, whichever is higher. It further states that where chair of the BOD and chief executive officer (CEO) are the same person, or the CEO is not an independent director, nonexecutive members should be a majority. |
| Number of independent directors | No. 1(2)(a) provides that at least one-fifth of the total number of board members shall be independent. | Independent directors shall be less than two or one-third of the total members of the BOD, whichever is higher (Regulation 6 of the Code). | Per Section 86(3), BOD shall have at least one independent director; where BOD has more than seven members, two independent directors. | Per A.5.2 of the Code, where the BOD has three nonexecutive directors, they should all be independent. Otherwise, three or two-thirds of the total members of BOD, whichever is higher, must be independent directors. |
| Definition of independence | Defined in No. 1(2) | Section 166(2) of the Act provides the definition. | Definition is provided in Section 89(2) | Definition is provided in A.5.3. Conditions factors relating to independence of a director are listed in A.5.5 |

continued on next page

*Table 8 continued*

| Key Point | Bangladesh | Pakistan | Nepal | Sri Lanka |
|---|---|---|---|---|
| Separation of role of chairman of BOD and CEO | No. 1(4)(a) has separated the role of chair of BOD and CEO ensuring that the posts must be held by different individuals. | Regulation 9 of the Code makes it an express requirement that chair of BOD and CEO shall not be the same person. | No provision made by the Act. However, the Listed Corporate Governance Directive, 2018, issued by Securities Board of Nepal, which is a binding directive, prohibits both positions, CEO and chair of BOD, to be held by the same person. | The Code, by virtue of A.2.1 allows for the roles of chair of BOD and CEO to be held by a single person, some qualification. |
| Committees of the Board | **Succession Planning**<br>No provision has been made for a committee dedicated to this task.<br><br>**Internal Controls and the appointment/supervision of the external auditor**<br>No. 4(i) read with No. 5(1)(a) stipulate that there shall be an Audit Committee which shall have the duty to monitor internal audit and compliance process, approve the internal audit and compliance plan, and also review the internal audit and compliance report (No. 5(5)(c)). Further, the Audit Committee shall also oversee hiring and monitor the performance of the external auditors (No. 5[5][d]). | **Succession Planning**<br>Regulation 29 of the Code provides for the creation of the Nomination Committee and Regulation 28 provides for the creation of the Human Resources and Remuneration (HR&R) Committee. The Nomination Committee is tasked with making recommendations to the board regarding the composition of committees of the board (Regulation 29[2][i] of the Code). The HR&R Committee is responsible for succession planning and performance evaluation of key executive personnel (Regulation 28[6][iv] of the Code).<br><br>**Internal Controls and the appointment/supervision of the external auditor**<br>Regulation 27 of the Code provides for the creation of the Audit Committee which shall be tasked with making recommendations to BOD regarding the appointment external auditors, removal, and other matters. A separate Risk Management Committee is provided for, for the purpose of internal audit activities (Regulation 30 of the Code). | **Succession Planning**<br>No provision is made under the Act.<br><br>**Internal Controls and the appointment/supervision of the external auditor**<br>Section 164 of the Act provides for the creation of an Audit Committee.<br><br>**Executive Remuneration**<br>No provision is made under the Act | **Succession Planning**<br>A.7.1 provides for the establishing of a Nomination Committee which shall make recommendations to BOD on all new BOD appointments.<br><br>**Internal Controls and the appointment/supervision of the external auditor**<br>D.3.1 provides for the establishment of an Audit Committee.<br><br>**Executive Remuneration**<br>B.1.1 provides for the establishment of a Remuneration Committee. The required composition of each committee is also provided for in each of their respective provisions. |

*continued on next page*

*Table 8 continued*

| Key Point | Bangladesh | Pakistan | Nepal | Sri Lanka |
|---|---|---|---|---|
| | **Executive Remuneration** | **Executive Remuneration** | | |
| | No. 4(ii) read with No. 6(1)(a) provide for the creation of the Nomination and Remuneration Committee. Responsibilities of the committee include formulating criteria to determine qualifications, positive attributes, and independence of a director, and thereby recommend a policy to BOD regarding the remuneration of the directors and top-level executive (No. 6[5]). | Regulation 28(6)(i) of the Code states that the HR&R Committee shall recommend a policy framework to BOD for determining remuneration of executive as well as nonexecutive directors. | | |
| Board Diversity | No provision exists which stipulates a mandatory diversity quota. However, the Nomination and Remuneration Committee is under obligation to devise a policy on board diversity (No. 6[5][b][ii]). | Regulation 4 of the Code require there to be at least one woman on the BOD. In the case of public interest companies, Section 154 of the Act requires the appointment of female representation on the BOD as may be prescribed by the Securities and Exchange Commission of Pakistan. | No provision made for gender quota. | No express requirement is made for gender quota. However, Schedule A states that the Nomination Committee shall regularly review the composition of the Board including gender representation. |

Note:

[1] The number of directors on the board has to be between five and 20 members (No. 1(1)). In the Draft Code of Corporate Governance 2012, the number of executive members was limited to two thus, automatically ensuring a majority of the nonexecutive members on the board.

Source: Authors.

# Bibliography

Adams, R. and T. Kirchmaier. 2012. Barriers to Boardrooms. *European Corporate Governance Institute (ECGI) -Finance Working Paper* No. 347/2013.

Adams, R. and T. Kirchmaier. 2016. Women on Boards in Finance and STEM Industries. *American Economic Review* 106 (5): 277-281.

Adams, R. and T. Kirchmaier. 2016. Women in Finance. *ECGI-Finance Working Paper* No. 479/2016.

Adams, R. B. 2005. What do Boards do? Evidence from Board Committee and Director Compensation Data (13 March 2003). *EFA 2005 Moscow Meetings Paper*.

De Haas, R., D. Ferreira and T. Kirchmaier, 'The Inner Workings of the Board: Evidence from Emerging Markets'. *Emerging Markets Review* (forthcoming).

Ferreira, D. and T. Kirchmaier. 2013. Corporate Boards in Europe: Size, Independence and Gender Diversity." In *Governing Corporate Europe Post-Crisis. Facts, Context and Reforms*, ed. M. Belcredi and G. Ferrarini, Cambridge: Cambridge University Press.

Kirchmaier, T. and G. Owen. 2008. The Changing Role of the Chairman. *European Business Organization Law Review (EBOR)*, 9:187-213.

Owen, G., T. Kirchmaier and J. Grant. 2006. *Corporate Governance in the US and Europe: Where Are We Now?* Palgrave Macmillan.

Puchniak, D., H. Baum, and L. Nottage. 2017. *Independent Directors in Asia*. Cambridge University Press.

Reeb, D. and A. Upadhyay. 2010. Subordinate board structures. *Journal of Corporate Finance*, Vol. 16, No. 4: 469–486.

Thomsen, S. and M. Conyon. 2019. *Corporate Governance and Board Decisions*. Djøf Forlag.

# STATE-OWNED ENTERPRISES

## Introduction

Corporate governance in state-owned enterprises (SOEs) presents particular challenges since the presence of a large shareholder that does not necessarily always pursue wealth-maximizing goals shifts the main agency conflict that regulation has to address from the relationship between shareholders and executives to that between majority and minority shareholders, with the additional complication that the decisions of the majority shareholder—the state—may not (only) be a function of business considerations, but (also) wider political or societal concerns. The relevance of this issue cannot be overstated: foreign direct investment will be in the form of the acquisition of minority stakes in domestic companies, including SOEs, and hence require legal assurances that the state as majority shareholder will respect the (financial) interests of the minority, and will not engage in the extraction of private benefits of control nor use their influence to pursue other (nonprofit maximizing) goals. This is a concern for both the private sector and multilateral development agencies that are typically heavily invested in a country's SOE sector.

This chapter assesses the prevalence of SOEs in, and their importance for, the domestic economy or particular sectors of the economy in a subset of South Asian Association for Regional Cooperation (SAARC) member countries (Bangladesh, Nepal, Pakistan, and Sri Lanka). It examines legal mechanisms used to retain control (majority stake or control-enhancing mechanisms such as "golden shares" or pyramidal structures[45]); management system used to exercise control; legal safeguards, if any, employed to ensure that government interference in operational decision-making is limited; and corporate governance mechanisms functioning as a safeguard against government interference, notably a requirement to have a strong independent element on the board, defined as including independence from the major shareholders, not only from management.

Each country section starts with an overview of the economic importance and financial performance of SOEs, describes the regulatory regime under which they operate, and assesses the legal mechanisms that determine the corporate governance of SOEs and constrain government interference in operational decision-making. The regulatory framework will then be benchmarked against the Organisation for Economic Co-operation and Development (OECD) Guidelines on Corporate Governance of State-Owned Enterprises and two national governance models: Singapore and the United Kingdom (UK). Singapore deserves particular attention because its SOEs are commercially highly successful, while the involvement of the government in corporate affairs is restricted to certain

---

[45] Golden shares grant control rights such as super-voting rights or a veto power to the holder. Pyramidal structures use the staggering of corporations to control the ultimate operating business with a relatively small voting bloc.

clearly defined, non-operational governance matters at a constitutional level. The UK was chosen as an additional comparator in order to include a perspective from a developed economy outside of the South Asian economic and cultural context, which has a legal system that is sufficiently close to South Asian jurisdictions to be of relevance to the present study.

# Governance of State-Owned Enterprises

## Existing International and Regional Initiatives

OECD has produced the detailed Guidelines on Corporate Governance of State-Owned Enterprises (OECD 2015),[46] which contain high-level principles, for example on the "equitable treatment" of all shareholders and a high degree of transparency to be observed by SOEs. The role of SOE boards has to be clearly defined in legislation, and the composition of the board should allow the exercise of objective and independent judgment. Importantly, all board members, including any public official, should be nominated based on qualifications and have equivalent legal responsibilities, and mechanisms should be implemented to avoid conflicts of interest and to limit political interference in board processes. The guidelines further require that listed SOEs, and, where practical, also unlisted SOEs, should adhere to national corporate governance codes. All countries analyzed in this report, with the exception of Nepal, have adopted such a code. In addition, several countries have promulgated separate codes for SOEs and private listed companies.[47]

Certain regional initiatives exist, for example the OECD–Asia Network on Corporate Governance of State-Owned Enterprises,[48] which provides a forum for public and private sector representatives from 16 Asian economies to discuss approaches to the governance of SOEs and areas of reform. However, the membership of the OECD–Asia Network only partly overlaps with the membership of the SAARC.[49] There is no initiative that focuses on South Asia and takes account of the region's specific economic and legal environment.

## Selected National Frameworks

### Singapore

The governance framework applicable to SOEs in Singapore has received considerable attention, owing to the economic success of Singapore's state holding company, Temasek Holdings.[50] Notably, studies have shown that Singapore SOEs have higher valuations than non-SOEs and have better corporate governance practices (Cheng-Han et al. 2016). This success has been associated with Singapore's

---

46   OECD. OECD Guidelines on Corporate Governance of State-Owned Enterprises. https://www.oecd.org/corporate/guidelines-corporate-governance-soes.htm.

47   Of the countries surveyed here, Pakistan and Sri Lanka have produced corporate governance codes for SOEs. The codes are discussed in the country sections.

48   OECD. Corporate Governance of State-Owned Enterprises in Asia. https://www.oecd.org/corporate/corporategovernanceofstate-ownedenterprisesinasia.htm.

49   The following SAARC member countries regularly participate in the Asia SOE Network: Bangladesh, Bhutan, India, and Pakistan.

50   See, e.g., Milhaupt and Pargendler (2017). Temasek Holdings is an investment company incorporated under the Singapore Company Act that is wholly government-owned. It owns and manages the government's global portfolio of minority and majority investments.

governance model for SOEs, which heavily curtails the influence of government representatives on the board of both Temasek itself and Temasek portfolio companies.

As far as the level of Temasek itself is concerned, the constitution of Singapore imposes restrictions on the manner in which government officials can influence operational decisions in Temasek, and hence indirectly in its portfolio companies. Temasek is owned by the Ministry of Finance, but the ministry does not have any representative on Temasek's board and the appointment, reappointment, and removal of Temasek directors has to be approved by the President of Singapore.[51] The board of Temasek is directly accountable to the President for the revenue and expenditure of the company and requires the President's approval for transactions that draw on its accumulated reserves.[52] Further, Temasek's charter makes it clear that management decisions are taken on purely operational grounds and without government interference. The charter provides in relevant part:

"Our portfolio companies are guided and managed by their respective boards and management; we do not direct their business decisions or operations.

Similarly, our investment, divestment and other business decisions are directed by our Board and management. Neither the President of Singapore nor our shareholder, the Singapore Government, is involved in our business decisions."

As far as the level of the portfolio company is concerned, a corporate governance framework applies and that is intended to limit government interference. Importantly, the chair of the board and at least one-third of board members of listed companies must be independent directors (which includes independence from substantial shareholders), and a majority of the board must be composed of independent directors if the chair is not independent. In practice, a clear majority of directors of Temasek portfolio companies are independent (indeed, a higher majority than in non-Temasek companies [Chen 2016]). In addition, the chair and CEO must be separate persons, a requirement that is again followed strictly by portfolio companies.

### United Kingdom

In the UK, all government holdings in public corporations are vested in the UK Government Investments Limited (UKGI), a private limited company that is wholly owned by HM Treasury. UKGI currently manages investments in 17 entities, ranging from assets of importance for national security, such as air traffic control, to financial services firms that had to be bailed out during the financial crisis, notably the Royal Bank of Scotland.[53] The company is expected to manage the government's investments "in a commercial way" and exercise the rights attaching to the government's shareholdings accordingly.[54] UKGI is ultimately accountable to the Chancellor of the Exchequer and, indirectly, to Parliament, but the company runs its business largely autonomously, and the government has undertaken not to intervene in business operations save in exceptional circumstances in a framework agreement between the Treasury as owner and the company.[55]

---

[51]    Constitution of the Republic of Singapore, Art 22C.
[52]    Constitution of the Republic of Singapore, Art 22B.
[53]    UKGI (2018), pp. 18–20.
[54]    UKGI (2018), para 3.3.
[55]    UKGI (2018), paras 5.1, 6.15.

In the discussion of the corporate governance framework, this study again distinguishes between the level of UKGI, the government's holding company, and the portfolio companies. As regards the former, overall strategic direction and oversight in matters of risk management, governance, and internal control are provided by UKGI's board, which must be composed of a majority of independent, nonexecutive directors coming from the private sector.[56] The proportion of nonexecutive directors is typically significantly higher and currently all board members except the chief executive are nonexecutives.[57] Both the UK Corporate Governance Code and general company law apply to the role and responsibilities of the board. Decisions, therefore, have to be taken in accordance with the directors' statutory, common law, and fiduciary duties.[58] The board has to form a remuneration, audit and risk, nominations, and transactions committee (the latter advising HM Treasury on the stewardship of, and, where applicable, preparation and execution of disposal strategies for assets held by UKGI), with responsibilities that are laid down in the framework agreement.[59] Thus, while the Treasury as owner of the company naturally has control over all board appointments,[60] political influence is circumscribed by providing for clearly specified channels of accountability; granting the board autonomy in day-to-day decision-making; ensuring that the company is subject to general laws and regulations; and, importantly, requiring a majority of board members to be independent directors with private sector experience.

Corporate governance requirements at the level of the portfolio company depend on the statutory form of the company (that is, whether it is incorporated under the UK Companies Act 2006 or a different statute) and whether or not it is listed. In the latter case, the UK's general corporate governance framework applies, which imposes requirements as to board diversity and independence similar to the UKGI Framework Agreement.[61] Where the general framework does not apply, the corporate governance arrangements differ from company to company, but common denominators are a predominantly nonexecutive board, with nonexecutive directors recruited from the private sector, a separation of the roles of chair and CEO, and the establishment of committees of the board, such as an audit committee, composed of nonexecutive directors.

# National Approaches in South Asia

The following sections will give an overview of the prevalence of SOEs in the domestic economy of a sample of SAARC member countries and describe the governance of SOEs according to national law and practice, paying particular attention to checks on government interference in management decisions. In order to facilitate comparison of the national regimes with the OECD Guidelines on Corporate Governance of State-Owned Enterprises, this study paraphrases here the main corporate governance-related principles of the guidelines in relevant parts. The guidelines consist of main principles, supporting subguidelines, and annotations containing examples of, and recommendations for, implementation. Main guidelines are reproduced below, followed in bullet point form by a summary of the subguidelines and annotations, to the extent that the guidelines and subguidelines have a specific bearing on legal and regulatory aspects of internal corporate governance.

---

[56]    UKGI (2018), para 6.3.
[57]    UKGI (2019), p. 32.
[58]    UKGI (2018), para 5.1.
[59]    UKGI (2018). para 6.13.
[60]    UKGI (2018), para 6.3.
[61]    Chapter 1.

## Table 9: OECD Guidelines on Corporate Governance in State-Owned Enterprises

| Area | Summary of Guidelines and Subguidelines |
|---|---|
| The state's role as an owner | The state should act as an informed and active owner, ensuring that the governance of state-owned enterprises (SOEs) is carried out in a transparent and accountable manner, with a high degree of professionalism and effectiveness.<br>• Governments should simplify and standardize the legal forms under which SOEs operate. Their operational practices should follow commonly accepted corporate norms.<br>• The government should allow SOEs full operational autonomy to achieve their defined objectives and refrain from intervening in SOE management. The government as a shareholder should avoid redefining SOE objectives in a nontransparent manner.<br>• The state should let SOE boards exercise their responsibilities and should respect their independence.<br>• The exercise of ownership rights should be clearly identified within the state administration. The exercise of ownership rights should be centralized in a single ownership entity, or, if this is not possible, carried out by a coordinating body. |
| SOEs in the marketplace | Consistent with the rationale for state ownership, the legal and regulatory framework for SOEs should ensure a level playing field and fair competition in the marketplace when SOEs undertake economic activities.<br>• Stakeholders and other interested parties, including creditors and competitors, should have access to efficient redress through unbiased legal or arbitration processes when they consider that their rights have been violated.<br>• SOEs undertaking economic activities should not be exempt from the application of general laws, tax codes, and regulations. |
| Equitable treatment of shareholders and other investors | Where SOEs are listed or otherwise include non-state investors among their owners, the state and the enterprises should recognize the rights of all shareholders, and ensure shareholders' equitable treatment and equal access to corporate information.<br>• The state should strive toward full implementation of the OECD Principles of Corporate Governance.<br>• Transactions between the state and SOEs, and between SOEs, should take place on market consistent terms.<br>• National corporate governance codes should be adhered to by all listed and, where practical, unlisted SOEs.<br>• Where SOEs are required to pursue public policy objectives; adequate information about these should be available to non-state shareholders at all times. |
| Stakeholder relations and responsible business | The state ownership policy should fully recognize SOEs' responsibilities toward stakeholders and request that SOEs report on their relations with stakeholders. It should make clear any expectations the state has in respect of responsible business conduct by SOEs.<br>• Listed or large SOEs should report on stakeholder relations.<br>• The boards of SOEs should develop, implement, monitor, and communicate internal controls, ethics, and compliance programs or measures, including those which contribute to preventing fraud and corruption. |
| Disclosure and transparency | SOEs should observe high standards of transparency and be subject to the same high-quality accounting, disclosure, compliance, and auditing standards as listed companies.<br>• SOEs should report material financial and nonfinancial information on the enterprise in line with high-quality internationally recognized standards of corporate disclosure, including:<br>  – enterprise financial and operating results;<br>  – governance, ownership, and voting structure of the enterprise;<br>  – the content of any corporate governance code or policy and implementation processes;<br>  – the remuneration of board members and key executives;<br>  – board member qualifications, selection process, and board diversity policies;<br>  – any financial assistance received from the state; and<br>  – any material transactions with the state and other related entities.<br>• Financial statements should be subject to an independent external audit based on high-quality standards. |

*continued on next page*

*Table 9  continued*

| Area | Summary of Guidelines and Subguidelines |
|------|------------------------------------------|
| The responsibilities of the boards of SOEs | The boards of SOEs should have the necessary authority, competencies, and objectivity to carry out their functions of strategic guidance and monitoring of management. They should act with integrity and be held accountable for their actions. <br>• The boards of SOEs should be assigned a clear mandate and ultimate responsibility for the enterprise's performance. <br>• Boards should have the power to appoint and remove the chief executive officer (CEO). They should set executive remuneration levels that are in the long-term interest of the enterprise. <br>• Board composition should allow the exercise of objective and independent judgment. All board members, including any public officials, should be nominated based on qualifications and have equivalent legal responsibilities. <br>• Independent board members, where applicable, should be free of any material interests or relationships with the enterprise, its management, other major shareholders, and the ownership entity that could jeopardize their exercise of objective judgment. <br>• Mechanisms should be implemented to avoid conflicts of interest preventing board members from objectively carrying out their board duties and to limit political interference in board processes. <br>• Good practice calls for the chair to be separate from the CEO. |

Source: Organisation for Economic Co-operation and Development (OECD).

## Bangladesh

### Economic Relevance

SOEs have played, and continue to play, a vital role in contributing to the economic development of Bangladesh. According to the Bangladesh Economic Review, a publication of the Ministry of Finance, there are currently about 50 public state-owned corporations in Bangladesh, which operate in a wide range of sectors, including manufacturing, power, gas and water, transport and communication, trade, agriculture, construction, and services.[62] Their total operating revenue is sizable, amounting to about 6% of gross domestic product (GDP). However, SOEs are generally not profitable, generating an aggregate net loss of Tk4,324.75 ($510 million) in the most recent financial year, and are heavily indebted, with outstanding commercial bank loans against 30 SOEs totaling Tk39,834.58 ($4.7 billion) (footnote 62). Private sector publications assess the financial position of SOEs equally negatively. The Financial Express reported in June 2019 that SOE losses were expected to rise to Tk56.7 billion ($670 million) in the next fiscal year.[63] It is difficult to obtain precise, authoritative figures, as no comprehensive statistics of state-owned companies are available.

Commentators consider SOEs to be a burden on the economy (footnote 63). They mention the limited working capital of SOEs; inadequate electricity supply, old factories; lack of BMRE (balancing, modernization, rehabilitation, and expansion) investments; weak management; and insufficiency of high-quality raw materials as reasons for the underperformance. In a competitive market, SOEs tend to lose market share to foreign producers or the private sector, which offers cheaper and better products (footnote 71).

---

[62]  Ministry of Finance, Bangladesh Economic Review (2019), Chapter 9: State-owned Enterprises.
[63]  *The Financial Express*. 2019. SoEs on track to rack up Tk 56b losses next fiscal. 17 June. https://thefinancialexpress.com.bd/economy/bangladesh/soes-on-track-to-rack-up-tk-56b-losses-next-fiscal-1560743641.

### Governance

SOEs are formed by President's Order or act of Parliament and controlled by different ministries of the Government of Bangladesh, depending on the sector in which they operate. Their governance structure is laid down in the respective order or act, and hence is not necessarily in line with general company law or, indeed, one uniform governance model. Typically, the board of directors has close links with the government and independent directors are in the minority. A good example is provided by the Bangladesh Shipping Corporation, which was formed by President's Order in 1972,[64] later repealed and replaced by the Bangladesh Shipping Corporation Act, 2017. Section 18(5) of the act states that not less than 51% of the paid-up share capital shall be owned by the government and the remaining shares may be offered for public subscription on the basis of a decision of the board of directors. Section 6(2) of the act determines the composition of the board of directors as follows:

The Board of Directors of the Corporation shall consists of not exceeding 13 members as follows:

- (i)     Minister, Ministry of Shipping, who shall also be its Chair;
- (ii)    Secretary, Ministry of Shipping, ex-officio;
- (iii)   one person not below the rank of a Joint-Secretary nominated by the Finance Division;
- (iv)   one person not below the rank of a Joint-Secretary nominated by the Ministry of Commerce;
- (v)    Managing Director of the Corporation, ex-officio;
- (vi)   Executive Director (Finance) of the Corporation, ex-officio;
- (vii)  Executive Director (Technical) of the Corporation, ex-officio;
- (viii) Executive Director (Commercial) of the Corporation, ex-officio;
- (ix)   Director or Directors elected by the shareholders provided that if the capital subscribed by the public exceeds 20% of total shares subscribed but not 34%, One director shall be appointed and where the capital subscribed exceeds 34%, two directors; and
- (x)    at least one independent Director nominated by the Government in accordance with the provisions made by the Bangladesh Securities and Exchange Commission, i.e., in accordance with the Corporate Governance Code, 2018.

### Legal Mechanisms to Limit Government Interference

Independent directors are appointed to the boards of both financial and nonfinancial SOEs with a view to ensuring that management decisions are taken in the commercial interest of the company. However, due to the direct involvement of officials from the government and the fact that independent nonexecutive directors are generally in the minority, the observations from independent directors are not always followed.

Section 4 of the Public Corporations (Management Coordination) Ordinance, 1986 provides for the formation of a council with the authority to act or take measures to ensure coordination and better management of public corporations, specifically to ensure that management decisions are taken in favor of the corporation. For example, the council has the power to approve production targets and profit and performance criteria for any public corporation, approve the declaration of dividends or the contribution of profits to the government, or coordinate management objectives of public corporations. However, the ordinance does not contain any provisions concerning the corporate

---

[64]    Bangladesh Shipping Corporation Order, 1972 (President's Order No. 10 of 1972).

governance of SOEs, and the composition of the council itself makes it clear that the council is a political institution that is composed entirely of government appointees.[65] At the time of writing, no information could be found about whether or how this council functions in practice.

The Office of the Comptroller and Auditor General (CAG) audits all statutory corporations and commercial enterprises in which the government owns 50% or more of the shares. CAG audit reports are delivered to the Public Accounts Committee (PAC) of the Parliament. The PAC has authority to take actions based on the CAG audit report. However, Sobhan and Werner (2003) point out that neither the CAG nor the PAC work effectively due to a lack of accountability and a shortage of qualified staff. In addition, the fact that these institutions only oversee the accounts, and the government as majority owner does not exercise effective oversight of financial management and governance matters, means that structural problems that give rise to underperformance have not yet been addressed.

In summary, in Bangladesh, SOE governance does not work effectively for several reasons. First and foremost, there is no effective system of oversight that would ensure that action is taken in the case of irregularities or underperformance, and no incentives exist that link reward to performance. Second, appointment decisions at the level of senior management and also at lower levels are often not driven by qualification and experience, but by political loyalty and influence. Third, decision-making procedures are long and cumbersome, given that the boards of SOEs often include representatives from several ministries. Fourth, government interference in the price-setting mechanism makes it difficult for SOEs to be run commercially and make profits. Finally, the mindset is frequently such that SOEs "do not see themselves as corporate enterprises and therefore see no need for corporate governance norms."[66]

## Nepal

### Economic Relevance

Currently 40 state-owned enterprises SOEs (also referred to as "public enterprises" or PEs) exist in Nepal, 37 of them pursuing commercial activities.[67] These enterprises have contributed 11%–14% to GDP since 2012.[68] The government plans to enlarge the public enterprise sector further, as it is felt that crucial investments cannot or will not be undertaken by the private sector.[69] However, financial performance of SOEs is uneven at best, with one-fourth to one-third of SOEs having been loss-making in recent financial years and about half having no accumulated profit.[70] The Ministry of Finance stated that "financial efficiency and effectiveness of ... most ... PEs [did] not seem to [have] increased as expected, only a limited number published audited financial statements, and significant improvement

---

[65]  Public Corporations (Management Coordination) Ordinance, 1986, s. 5. Pursuant to s. 6 of the Ordinance, the Council has the authority to appoint a committee of experts that may provide the Council with research services, offer advice on professional or technical matters concerning public corporations, or assist in the performance evaluation of SOEs. However, decision authority lies with the government representatives who are the Council's members.

[66]  F. Sobhan and W. Werner, eds. 2003. A Comparative Analysis of Corporate Governance in South Asia: Charting a Roadmap for Bangladesh. Bangladesh Enterprise Institute. p. 27.

[67]  Ministry of Finance. Annual Performance Review of Public Enterprises 2018, p. 1.

[68]  Footnote 67, pp. 5–6.

[69]  Footnote 67, p. 2.

[70]  Footnote 67, p. 4.

[was] required to maintain their fiscal discipline."[71] Similarly, the government acknowledged that management procedures in PEs lacked adequate professionalism, autonomy, and control.[72]

### Governance

The majority of SOEs have been established under the general Nepalese companies legislation, the Companies Act, 2063 (2006),[73] while about one-fourth have been formed under special acts of Parliament. Their governance structure, processes to appoint managers and directors, and operating procedures, accordingly, differ widely. It has been pointed out that there is no common understanding to whom managers are accountable: the board of directors, shareholders, the line ministry, or the Ministry of Finance. Internal control structures are not well developed and accountability is weak.[74] The governance problems are compounded by the fact that no single agency has been made responsible for monitoring SOEs and ensuring that high corporate governance standards are implemented. Responsibilities are shared between the Ministry of Finance, which has certain monitoring tasks, and the relevant sector ministries, which typically nominate the chief executive, have representatives on the boards of SOEs, and often interfere intensively in operational decisions. However, there is no clear delineation of responsibilities or allocation of tasks between the ministries and, as a consequence, no effective exercise of ownership rights by the government (footnote 74).

### Legal Mechanisms to Limit Government Interference

The Corporation Coordination Division of the Ministry of Finance monitors the performance of SOEs and sets annual operational targets, which are published in a "yellow book." As part of its terms of reference, division also seeks to improve corporate governance standards, pay structures, and management practices in PEs, and has established guidelines and criteria governing the appointment of CEOs. However, its recommendations do not seem to be implemented consistently, and the authority of the line ministry to give directions to the enterprises falling within their remit is largely unfettered in practice. Supervisory activity is also hampered by staff shortages and insufficient technical expertise.[75]

The main external mechanism to control the expenditure incurred by PEs is the Auditor General of Nepal, who has the authority to audit the accounts of wholly owned SOEs pursuant to Article 241 of the Constitution of Nepal and s. 6 of the Audit Act, 2048 (1991). However, the Auditor General does not serve as an adequate substitute for weak regulatory safeguards against government interference in commercial operations. First, it is not sufficient for the Auditor General to be only in charge of the audit of wholly owned public enterprises, but not other PEs where the government has 51% or more ownership. Second, as has been observed in a country report compiled by the International Monetary Fund (2007), the level of staffing of the Auditor General and the technical skills of the staff are currently inadequate to ensure an effective audit of PEs.

---

[71]   Footnote 67, p. 4.
[72]   Footnote 67, p. 32.
[73]   Available at http://www.ocr.gov.np/images/pdf/the-companies-act%202006-english.pdf.
[74]   Ministry of Finance. Annual Performance Review of Public Enterprises 2018, p. 33.
[75]   International Monetary Fund (IMF). 2007. Nepal: Report on Observance of Standards and Codes. *IMF Country Report* No. 07/346.

## Pakistan

### Economic Relevance

Figures published by the Ministry of Finance of the Government of Pakistan show that just over 200 SOEs exist in Pakistan. Of this number, 138 are commercial corporations that contribute about 10% to GDP.[76] Most SOEs are engaged in the provision of essential infrastructure and related services, including electricity, gas, airports, railways, financial services, industry, and engineering.[77] Some of the major, and most important, companies in Pakistan are SOEs. Total market capitalization of SOEs is around 28%, and three of the 25 largest companies listed on the Pakistan Stock Exchange in 2017 were SOEs.[78] The amount of investment of the government in SOEs is also substantial. The total asset base of the federal government's SOE portfolio increased from PRs14.5 trillion ($94 billion) in fiscal year (FY) 2015/16 to PRs17.1 trillion ($110 billion) in FY 2016/17.[79]

The economic importance of SOEs, however, is not matched by their financial success. The net profit of commercial SOEs alone is negative, with losses totaling PRs12 billion ($77 million) in FY 2016/17, according to government figures (not accounting for noncommercial SOEs such as transport authorities).[80] There is a growing call for the reform of SOEs, aimed at less government interference and more independence.[81] Importantly, a case is pending before the Lahore High Court over the legality of the formation of certain provincial SOEs.[82]

Reasons for the poor performance of SOEs are seen in weak governance structures, excessive staff recruitment, political interference, and a lack of familiarity with business practices and market demands. Further, the change of power from one political party to another after general elections leads to political appointments which are perceived to have adverse effects on the decision-making process of SOEs (footnote 82).

### Governance

A public sector company (i.e., an SOE) is defined as "a company, whether public or private, which is directly or indirectly controlled, beneficially owned or not less than fifty-one percent of the voting securities or voting power of which are held by the Government or any instrumentality or agency of the Government or a statutory body, or in respect of which the Government or any instrumentality or agency of the Government or a statutory body, has otherwise power to elect, nominate or appoint [a] majority of its directors."[83] SOEs can be created either by a special act of Parliament or registration

---

[76]   Ministry of Finance. Federal Footprint–SOE Annual Report, FY2017, pp. 9, 17.
[77]   Footnote 76, p. 30.
[78]   List available at www.psx.com.pk/psx/themes/psx/uploads/Top_Companies_for_the_year_2017.pdf. These three companies are: Fauji Fertiliser Company Limited, majority-owned by Fauji Foundation, which is an SOE; Sui Northern Gas Pipeline Limited, majority-owned by the President of Pakistan; and Mari Petroleum Company Limited, 40% owned by Fauji Foundation and 18.39% owned by the Government of Pakistan.
[79]   Footnote 76, p. 31.
[80]   Footnote 76, p. 19.
[81]   K. Khan. 2018. State-owned enterprises in Pakistan—a drain on the economy. *Daily Times.* 29 November. https://dailytimes.com.pk/327296/state-owned-enterprises-in-pakistan-a-drain-on-the-economy.
[82]   *Shan Saeed Ghumman vs Federation of Pakistan,* W.P No.112301/2017, Lahore High Court.
[83]   Companies Act, 2017, s. 2(54). The same definition can be found in Public Sector Companies (Corporate Governance) Rules 2013, as amended by S.R.O. No. 275(I)/2017, Rule 2(g).

under the general companies legislation. Most SOEs are incorporated under the Companies Ordinance 1984, the predecessor of the Companies Act, 2017.[84]

If an SOE is created by a special act of Parliament, this act will generally determine the governance structure of the company and the composition of the board of directors. The Pakistan Broadcasting Corporation may serve as an example for such a company. The broadcasting corporation was established by the Pakistan Broadcasting Corporation Act, 1973. Section 4 of the act states that the administration and general direction of the corporation shall vest in the board, and the structure of that board shall be as follows: The chair of the board shall be the Secretary to the Government of Pakistan, Ministry of Information and Media Department. The further board members shall include:

- one eminent person each from the four provinces relating to media and management to be appointed by the Federal Government;
- an additional Foreign Secretary;
- an additional Secretary Finance;
- the Director General, ISPR (Inter-Services Public Relations);
- the Managing Director, PTVC (Pakistan Television Corporation);
- the Director General, PBC (Pakistan Business Council); and
- a representative of the Interior Division.

If an SOE is established by the government under the Companies Act, 2017[85] (or, before its enactment, the Companies Ordinance 1984), it is registered as a company by the procedure stipulated under the Companies Act. The company is bound by the mandatory requirements of the Companies Act and, where it is listed and falls under the supervisory powers of the Securities and Exchange Commission of Pakistan (SECP), the SECP Act and the relevant rules and regulations promulgated under the Companies Act, 2017, and the SECP Act. In particular, such companies are bound by the Listed Companies (Code of Corporate Governance) Regulations, 2019, which establish minimum requirements concerning board diversity and independence.[86]

In addition, all public sector companies as defined above,[87] both listed and unlisted, have to comply with the Public Sector Companies (Corporate Governance) Rules 2013 (the 2013 Rules), which provide for corporate governance rules specifically designed for SOEs.[88] In the case of a conflict with the requirements of the Corporate Governance Code for listed companies, the public sector rules prevail.[89] The 2013 Rules, importantly, require the board of a public sector company to consist of "executive and non-executive directors, including independent directors and those representing

---

84    Footnote 76, p. 10.
85    Government of Pakistan, Securities and Exchange Commission. ACT NO. XIX OF 2017 (Companies Act, 2017). https://www.secp.gov.pk/document/companies-act-2017/?wpdmdl=28472.
86    Government of Pakistan, Securities and Exchange Commission of Pakistan. Listed Companies (Code of Corporate Governance) Regulations, 2019. https://www.secp.gov.pk/document/listed-companies-code-of-corporate-governance-regulations-2019/?wpdmdl=36088. The regulations are discussed in detail in Chapter 1.
87    Text to Footnote 106.
88    Government of Pakistan, Securities and Exchange Commission of Pakistan. Public Sector Companies (Corporate Governance) Rules 2013. https://www.secp.gov.pk/document/psc-rules-as-amended-upto-april-21-2017/?wpdmdl=27850.
89    Public Sector Companies (Corporate Governance) Rules 2013, Rule 1(4).

minority interests with the requisite range of skills, competence, knowledge, experience and approach so that the Board as a group includes core competencies and diversity considered relevant in the context of the Public Sector Company's operations."[90] Further, at least one-third of the board members must be independent.[91] Thus, the 2013 Rules (and other applicable laws and regulations) do not change the fact that the relevant ministry controls an SOE through a majority of government appointees (executive as well as nonexecutive) on the board, and accordingly has the power to appoint the chief executive officer (CEO) of the company pursuant to the Companies Act, 2017.[92] It should also be noted that the chair, who should not be identical with the CEO pursuant to the 2013 Rules,[93] may be appointed by the government and does not have to be an independent director.[94] The rules, so far as they go, seem to be implemented fairly consistently in practice, although not without exceptions. The government reports that 26% of directors in SOEs are independent, thus below the required threshold of one-third.[95]

Further, it is important to note, and has been mentioned by the Government of Pakistan as a deficiency of the current system, that no centralized holding structure exists. Instead, SOEs are controlled by one or more ministries with responsibility for the sector in which the SOE operates. Thus, channels of oversight and accountability are unclear and operational decision-making is often influenced by potentially conflicting political objectives.[96]

### Legal Mechanisms to Limit Government Interference

Two mechanisms serve as a check on government interference in the management of SOEs: the Auditor General of Pakistan and the general requirements of company law and securities regulation.

First, the Constitution, pursuant to Article 169, and the Auditor General's (Functions, Powers, and Terms and Conditions or Service) Ordinance, 2001, pursuant to Section 8, empower the Auditor General of Pakistan to conduct an audit of all expenditures by all authorities and bodies established by the federal and/or the provincial governments. Thus, the Auditor General is, in principle, able to inspect SOEs and intervene where expenditure has been incurred in violation of applicable laws. However, for a variety of reasons ranging from a lack of financial, technological, and human resources, to a lack of cooperation by audited firms, audits of SOEs (and more generally, government audits) are perceived as not being effective.[97]

Second, general company law, such as directors' duties, apply to both SOEs registered under the Companies Act, 2017 (or the Companies Ordinance 1984) and SOEs created by special enactment. If funds are misapplied, directors may therefore be liable for compensation, although litigation will

---

90   Public Sector Companies (Corporate Governance) Rules 2013, Rule 3(1).
91   Public Sector Companies (Corporate Governance) Rules 2013, Rule 3(2). Pursuant to Rule 2(1)(d), an independent director is defined as 'a Non-Executive Director who is not in the service of Pakistan or of any statutory body or any body or institution owned or controlled by the Government, and who is not connected or does not have any other relationship, whether pecuniary or otherwise, with the Public Sector Company, its associated companies, subsidiaries, holding company or directors.'
92   Companies Act, 2017, ss. 186, 187.
93   Public Sector Companies (Corporate Governance) Rules 2013, Rule 4(1).
94   Public Sector Companies (Corporate Governance) Rules 2013, Rule 4(4).
95   Footnote 76, p. 14.
96   Footnote 76, p. 27.
97   A. Masood and R. N. Lodhi. 2015. Factors Affecting the Success of Government Audits: A Case Study of Pakistan. *Universal Journal of Management* 52.

arguably only occur in cases of clear noncompliance.[98] If the SOE is not wholly owned, and government interference in the business operations of the company is such as to be oppressive to the interests of outside investors, the minority shareholders can also file a winding up petition in the High Court under Section 301 of the Companies Act, 2017.

In addition to the Companies Act, 2017, the Public Sector Companies (Corporate Governance) Rules 2013 impose a variety of requirements on the conduct of the management of an SOE. Importantly, the 2013 Rules establish an approval process for related-party transactions,[99] which must be placed before the audit committee of the company and, upon recommendation of the audit committee, reviewed and approved by the board.[100] Given that the majority of directors on the board of SOEs are often executives and nonexecutives affiliated with the government, it may, however, be questioned whether board review and approval constitutes an effective safeguard against conflicted transactions.

### Sri Lanka

#### Economic Relevance

SOEs play an important role in the economy of Sri Lanka, contributing around 13%–14% to total GDP and being particularly prominent in strategic sectors, including energy, water, ports, banking and insurance, transportation, aviation, and construction.[101] More than 400 SOEs operate in Sri Lanka; 54 of these are currently designated "strategically important State Owned Businesses Enterprises (SOBEs)" that are regarded as central in transforming the country's economy and fostering growth (footnote 101). Most of the sector's contribution to GDP stems from these enterprises. However, performance of SOBEs is not consistently good; return on assets is generally very low and, in some years, the sector is overall loss-making.[102] SOBEs, therefore, are perceived as not performing to their full potential.[103] According to the government, reasons for the unsatisfactory performance include lack of good governance practices and no clear accountability, inadequate policy and legal frameworks, and weak supervision by the relevant institutions (footnote 103). This negative perception is shared by commentators and the public, in general.[104] A landmark report has described the existing internal control, monitoring, and governance frameworks as inadequate; underperformance as common; and fraud, mismanagement, corruption, and negligence as a function of "deeper, structural weaknesses,

---

[98]  In at least one decision, Human Rights Case No. 3654 of 2018 (In the matter regarding appointment of Managing Director, Pakistan Television Corporation), the managing director of a public sector company, Pakistan Television Corporation, was found liable for a breach of his duties where funds were used for purposes not in line with the company's objectives. See Corporate Governance Frameworks for more details.

[99]  The term "related parties" is not defined in the 2013 Rules, and instead the general definition under the Companies Act, 2017, applies (see Public Sector Companies [Corporate Governance] Rules 2013, Rule 2[2]). The general definition captures transactions between the company and another SOE (which qualify as associated companies within the meaning of the Companies Act, 2017).

[100]  Public Sector Companies (Corporate Governance) Rules 2013, Rule 9.

[101]  Department of Public Enterprises. Performance Report 2018, p. 1.

[102]  This was the case, for example, in 2018, see Department of Public Enterprises. Performance Report 2018, p.1. A comparison of the revenue generated for, and financial support received from, the government paints a similar picture. In 2018, income for the treasury in the form of levies and dividend payments amounted to PRs42 billion, while SOEs received PRs73 billion as a transfer from the national budget for restructuring and the expansion of business activities (Department of Public Enterprises. Performance Report 2018, p. 4).

[103]  Department of Public Enterprises. Performance Report 2017, p. 1.

[104]  Daily FT, 12 June 2019: State-Owned Enterprises' losses double. http://www.ft.lk/top-story/State-Owned-Enterprises--losses-double/26-679833.

rather than isolated incidents of opportunistic behavior by individuals or occasional lapses in control, resulting in a "dysfunctional state that serves political interests."[105]

## Governance

SOEs are either public corporations or so-called statutory boards (universities, hospitals, and other public institutes and agencies) that are incorporated under a special or general act of Parliament and carry out public functions, or companies registered under the Companies Act 2007 with a majority of the share capital being held by the government.[106] Most SOEs are monitored by the Public Enterprise Department of the Ministry of Finance, which also issues guidelines and circulars to improve corporate governance in SOEs, while some fall within the purview of the Department of National Budget. In addition, the relevant line ministries also retain powers to intervene in business matters.[107] Parliamentary control is mainly exerted through the Committee on Public Enterprises. The Department of Public Enterprises has produced a Code of Best Practice in Corporate Governance for Public Enterprises, which is intended to strengthen the accountability, transparency, and internal controls of commercially operating public enterprises.[108] The code will be discussed in more detail in the next section. For other SOEs not covered by the Code of Best Practice, the Ministry of Finance published a different set of (less demanding) guidelines, entitled "Public Enterprises Guidelines for Good Governance."[109]

## Legal Mechanisms to Limit Government Interference

The Code of Best Practice in Corporate Governance for Public Enterprises defines the relationship between the government and the public enterprise and lays down how the government can influence operational decisions in SOEs. Among other matters, the code provides, first, that each SOE should adopt a "corporate charter" (which is equivalent to the memorandum and articles of association under corporate law).[110] The corporate charter is prepared by the minister of finance in consultation with the responsible line minister and adopted by the SOE's shareholders in general meeting. Its function is not to override existing laws and regulations, but to complement the enabling legislation under which public enterprises are established in order to introduce decision-making and governance mechanisms comparable to those applicable to private sector companies under the Companies Act and Sri Lanka Corporate Governance Code.

Second, the code stipulates that government officials "entrusted with the rights and responsibilities of ownership and supervision over a Public Enterprise have a fiduciary duty to exercise these rights and responsibilities in an accountable and transparent manner, in good faith and in the best interests of the

---

[105] Advocata. 2019. *The State of State Enterprises in Sri Lanka.*

[106] A more technical definition is given by the Public Enterprises Guidelines for Good Governance, s. 1.1. The guidelines distinguish between a public corporation, meaning "any Corporation, Board or any other body which was or is established by or under any written law other than the Companies Act, with capital wholly or partly provided by the Government by way of grant, loan or other form," and a public enterprise, defined as "any public Corporation, Board or other body, which was or is established under any written law, including Companies Act, where the Government has the controlling interest."

[107] Footnote 105, p. 36.

[108] Government of Sri Lanka, Ministry of Finance. Code of Best Practice in Corporate Governance for Public Enterprises in Sri Lanka. http://www.treasury.gov.lk/documents/63940/182428/codeofbestpractice.pdf/107546ab-4ffc-4b83-b3a6-8ed0011d8859.

[109] Government of Sri Lanka, Ministry of Finance. Public Enterprises Guidelines for Good Governance. http://www.treasury.gov.lk/documents/63940/182428/guidelines.pdf/53c33d35-1f6d-4e78-81da-ad281304f1a4.

[110] Code of Best Practice in Corporate Governance for Public Enterprises in Sri Lanka, Section 4: Implementation Guidelines, s. 1.3.

enterprise and the public."[111] These fiduciary duties are intended to have the same meaning and effect as the duties and responsibilities that shareholders have under corporate law, although it does not seem to be the case that any such duties have in practice become a matter of a legal dispute and been enforced in court.[112]

Third, government officials "should be prohibited from interfering in the Board's and management's exercise of their mandated rights and responsibilities ... except on matters which are explicitly reserved for the Minister of Finance, the responsible Minister and officials as stipulated in the enterprise's Corporate Charter."[113] Directions, if any, should accordingly be given following normal channels of corporate law, i.e., the government as a shareholder is expected to table a resolution in general meeting (footnote 113).

Fourth, the code contains detailed provisions on the composition of the board of directors that mirror closely, and in some respects go beyond, the best practice standards of the Sri Lanka Corporate Governance Code 2017.[114] Boards should have a balance of executive and independent nonexecutive directors so that no individual or small group of individuals can dominate the board's decision-making.[115] Independent nonexecutive directors should comprise at least half, and preferably a majority of board members, and government officials should not be appointed to more than one-third of board seats.[116] The appointment process should be overseen by a nomination committee headed by an independent director. The nomination committee can consult and co-opt government officials to assist in the selection of candidates, but it is expected to recommend board appointments based on an open and competitive process.[117] Boards are further required to form audit and remuneration committees composed entirely of nonexecutive directors.[118]

These principles are sensible and take into account international best practice standards, including private sector initiatives such as the UK's Cadbury Code and subsequent corporate governance codes, and the OECD's Guidelines on Corporate Governance in SOEs. There are no official statistics on the extent to which the code has been adopted, or which principles have been implemented, but anecdotal evidence suggests that adoption is sporadic. Corporate governance disclosures even in the largest SOEs are frequently minimal and not in line with the requirements of the Code of Best Practice. It has also been observed by commentators that corporate structures are often obscure and transparency standards are low.[119]

# Conclusion

In most countries analyzed in this report, the SOE sector underperforms heavily and there is a perception that SOEs are generally inefficiently run and lack effective oversight and governance

---

[111]   Code of Best Practice in Corporate Governance for Public Enterprises in Sri Lanka, s. 2.2.
[112]   Code of Best Practice in Corporate Governance for Public Enterprises in Sri Lanka, s. 2.2.2.
[113]   Code of Best Practice in Corporate Governance for Public Enterprises in Sri Lanka, s. 2.3.
[114]   See Chapter 1.
[115]   Code of Best Practice in Corporate Governance for Public Enterprises in Sri Lanka, Section 4: Implementation Guidelines, s. 4.10.
[116]   Code of Best Practice in Corporate Governance for Public Enterprises in Sri Lanka, s. 4.10.1, 4.10.2.
[117]   Code of Best Practice in Corporate Governance for Public Enterprises in Sri Lanka, s. 4.11.
[118]   Code of Best Practice in Corporate Governance for Public Enterprises in Sri Lanka, ss. 4.12, 6.4.
[119]   Footnote 105, pp. 27–29.

structures. Often, governments themselves acknowledge the need for reform. The Pakistan government, for example, admitted that "overlapping ownership and management functions coupled with ... unclear and indefinite mandates have undermined [the] full efficiency [of SOEs]. To improve SOE performance, efforts must be taken to create an atmosphere where SOEs operate in an independent environment without any political affiliations and where a centralized, independent board regularly evaluates both the financial and nonfinancial performance."[120] This report underlines this assessment. If mapped against the OECD guidelines, it can be seen that current national regimes fall short along most dimensions.

**Table 10: National Approaches Benchmarked against OECD Guidelines**

| Area | National Approach |
|---|---|
| The state's role as an owner | For all countries surveyed, the following holds:<br>• Legal forms are not standardized.<br>• Operational autonomy is not fully safeguarded. There is some variation across countries, with no effective safeguards in Bangladesh, Nepal, and Sri Lanka, and certain corporate governance standards that are designed to limit government interference applied in Pakistan. However, even in Pakistan, implementation of the relevant standards is by no means uniform.<br>• No single ownership entity. |
| State-owned enterprises (SOEs) in the marketplace | • Redress for stakeholders and other interested parties: In some countries, limited avenues for redress exist and have been exploited (see, in particular, litigation in Pakistan), but generally there is no easily accessible, efficient mechanism for private parties to challenge the actions of SOEs or claim compensation for alleged breaches of duty.<br>• Certain exemptions from general laws exist for SOEs in all countries surveyed, but important concepts, such as directors' duties, generally apply. However, enforcement is virtually non-existent. |
| Equitable treatment of shareholders and other investors | • Some states (Pakistan, Sri Lanka) have developed corporate governance codes or guidelines specifically for the public sector, which are modeled to some extent after the OECD Principles of Corporate Governance. However, implementation is uneven across countries.<br>• Where corporate governance codes for SOEs exist (Pakistan and Sri Lanka), these codes employ the audit committee to monitor transactions between the state and the public enterprise. However, on the available data, it could not be ascertained whether the required procedures ensure that such transactions take place on an arm's length basis.<br>• National corporate governance codes for listed companies, where they exist, are applied to listed SOEs in the countries surveyed.<br>• Adequate information about public policy objectives, which SOEs are generally required to pursue in the countries surveyed, is often not available to non-state shareholders. |
| Stakeholder relations and responsible business | • In Pakistan, and Sri Lanka, applicable regulations contain requirements on internal controls and compliance. However, on the available data, it is unclear whether such controls are implemented consistently and how well they operate in practice. Reports in the financial press and by other commentators are generally highly critical of existing mechanisms to prevent mismanagement, fraud, and corruption. |
| Disclosure and transparency | • In all countries surveyed, SOEs are required to report financial and operating results. However, compliance with financial reporting requirements is uneven, and in some countries a sizable proportion of SOEs does not publish audited financial statements.<br>• Nonfinancial elements of disclosure required by the OECD guidelines (i.e., information on governance, ownership and voting structures, board member qualifications, selection process) are only disclosed in a minority of cases. |

*continued on next page*

120 Footnote 76, p. 27.

*Table 10  continued*

| Area | National Approach |
|------|-------------------|
| The responsibilities of the boards of SOEs | • The board is at least formally assigned ultimate responsibility for the enterprise's performance in all countries surveyed.<br>• Where corporate governance codes for SOEs exist (Pakistan and Sri Lanka), boards are expected to consist of a balance of executive and nonexecutive directors, and appointments should be made based on qualifications, rather than political affiliation. Boards are further required to include independent directors: in Pakistan a minority, in Sri Lanka at least half, preferably a majority. With the exception of Pakistan, there is no comprehensive data on implementation. In Pakistan, compliance, at least with the letter of the rules, is relatively high, albeit not universal.<br>• The roles of chief executive officer (CEO) and chair of the board of an SOE have to be separated in Pakistan and Sri Lanka.<br>• Generally, the government has at least de facto control over the appointment of the CEO. |

Source: Organisation for Economic Co-operation and Development (OECD).

In comparison with the two benchmark systems discussed in section 3.2.2, this report concludes that none of the countries surveyed has adopted a governance system for SOEs comparable with the Singapore or UK model, although some South Asian national policy makers refer to these countries as exemplars of best practice in the governance of SOEs.[121] In particular, the surveyed countries do not use a centralized holding structure or a uniform regulatory framework to govern SOEs. Governance standards, where they have been drafted specifically for SOEs, do not always take account of the particularities of the SOE sector (see third recommendation for more details). The effectiveness of control mechanisms is often further hampered by human resources constraints and a lack of technical expertise. Taking these issues into account, our main recommendations are as follows:

(i)  **Clear channels of accountability and responsibility:** Channels of accountability and—from the perspective of the government—responsibility for oversight, maintaining high corporate governance standards, and the exercise of ownership rights in the best interests of the company should be clearly defined. There should be one public body in charge of the above functions, and the multiplication of reporting channels and overlapping control, appointment, and veto or approval rights should be avoided. The importance of these features of an effective governance system of SOEs has been acknowledged by some governments surveyed in this study,[122] but regulatory reforms nevertheless seem to be difficult to implement, perhaps because of vested interests and complex political decision-making processes.

(ii)  **Uniform legal framework:** All SOEs should be subject to one set of rules and legal requirements, at least as far as SOEs are concerned that operate on commercial terms. To this effect, a sensible legal setup is the incorporation of SOEs under the general companies' legislation of a country, rather than special acts of Parliament. General directors' duties and other legal requirements should apply to boards of SOEs. Governments may produce a set of corporate governance rules specifically applicable to SOEs, as is the case in some of the countries surveyed for this study, since not all general corporate governance standards are suitable for the SOE sector.[123] However, these rules should apply without exception to all commercially operating SOEs, and their implementation should be supervised effectively, in

---

[121]  For example, Pakistan, see note 144.

[122]  Nepal Ministry of Finance. Annual Performance Review of Public Enterprises 2018, p. 35.

[123]  In particular, the definition of independence found in the general companies legislation or corporate governance code is not always suitable for present purposes, since it can be, and has been in some cases (see Pakistan, section 0 above), interpreted as not requiring independence from the government as majority shareholder.

order to ensure a level playing field and avoid confusion about the legal duties and obligations that govern the conduct of directors and officers.

(iii) **Safeguards to limit political interference in operational decision-making:** Political intervention in the day-to-day operations of SOEs should be limited through binding legal and/ or structural safeguards.

– A first mechanism, present in both Singapore and the UK, is the interposition of a holding company that exercises all ownership functions of the state. Regulatory reform can then focus on this holding company with a view to ensuring a high level of professionalism at the board and senior management level of the holding company. Laws or a legally binding agreement between the government and the holding company comparable to the framework agreement concluded between UK Government Investments Limited and the Treasury as the responsible government department should provide for a majority of private sector individuals with professional experience on the board of the holding company and clearly delineate the instances when, and the processes through which, the government is entitled to intervene in management matters.

– A second mechanism, also present in Singapore, is the concentration of ultimate powers of oversight and direction in the hands of one political body or, indeed, one person who is democratically directly accountable. As discussed in section 3.2.2 above, the President of Singapore has to approve the appointment, reappointment, and removal of all Temasek directors, the board of Temasek is accountable to the President for the revenue and expenditure of the company, and the President has the power to veto certain transactions. It is particularly useful to concentrate powers of oversight and direction at the highest level of government in political systems where democratic accountability is higher than bureaucratic efficiency, as measured, for example, by the World Bank Worldwide Governance Indicators.

– A third mechanism operates at the level of the portfolio company. Here, as at the level of the holding company (if any), regulation, for example a code of corporate governance for SOEs, should ensure that SOEs are run in a commercially efficient manner and in the best interest of the company and its shareholders, in particular where a SOE is not wholly owned by the government. With certain caveats (see second recommendation), best practice standards promulgated for private listed companies are in principle useful to achieve this goal. Notably, having a sizable number of independent directors on the board (ideally, a majority); the separation of chair and CEO, requiring the chair of the board to be independent; and establishing board committees for particularly sensitive areas of decision-making (traditionally internal control and audit, executive remuneration, and succession planning) are features of modern private sector corporate governance codes that should be retained for SOEs. In taking account of the specific institutional context of SOEs, these rules, however, should be amplified in several respects. First, as mentioned above (second recommendation), the definition of independence should include independence from the government. Second, a particular risk at government-controlled enterprises is the pursuit of investment projects that are not in the best commercial interest of the company. This may be defensible if ex ante clearly specified and appropriately disclosed public policy goals are pursued, but particular attention must be paid to the SOEs receiving value for money. In this regard, the internal audit function and the audit committee, or another board committee specifically constituted for this purpose, such as a related-party transactions committee, is of central importance. Public sector corporate governance standards should address this problem and provide for a governance solution, for example, by specifying that the responsibilities of the audit committee include implementing a value for money framework or requiring the establishment of a dedicated transactions committee. Third, the traditional enforcement mechanism of corporate governance codes is the so-called "comply or explain" model, which relies on financial markets to penalize companies that do not have effective governance structures, i.e., do not comply and also do not give a satisfactory explanation for their noncompliance. Since SOEs enterprises operate with an implicit or explicit guarantee by the government to commit funds when necessary, higher capital costs mediated by the financial markets do not have the same penalizing effect as for the private sector. For this reason, the relevant corporate governance rules should be mandatory.

(iv) **Enhancing institutional capacity:** Finally, in addition to regulatory reforms, enhancing institutional capacity is of paramount importance. This should happen at the level of both the enterprise and the holding company or other public body discharging oversight and ownership functions. At the level of the enterprise, it is necessary to enhance the professionalism of those responsible for internal management and control systems; awareness of the different roles, responsibilities, and legal duties of executive and nonexecutive directors; and compliance with reporting requirements and other legal obligations. At the level of the holding company or other responsible public body, it is necessary to embed a commercial approach and ensure that those with the authority to take decisions concerning the management and governance of portfolio companies have the necessary technical knowledge and are familiar with the relevant legal rules determining decisions at that level. The latter include general legal requirements applicable to majority shareholders and, if a holding company has been established, directors' duties and corporate governance standards.

# Bibliography

Advocata. 2019. *The State of State Enterprises in Sri Lanka.*

Chen, C. 2016. Solving the Puzzle of Corporate Governance of State-Owned Enterprises: The Path of the Temasek Model in Singapore and Lessons for China. 36 *Nw. J. Int'l L. & Bus.* 303

Cheng-Han, T., D. W. Puchniak, and U. Varottil. 2016. State-Owned Enterprises in Singapore: Historical Insights Into a Potential Model for Reform. 28 *Columbia Journal of Asian Law* 61.

International Monetary Fund (IMF). 2007. Nepal: Report on Observance of Standards and Codes. *IMF Country Report* No. 07/346.

Masood, A. and R. Lodhi. 2015. Factors Affecting the Success of Government Audits: A Case Study of Pakistan. 3 *Universal Journal of Management* 52.

Milhaupt, C. and M. Pargendler. 2017. Governance Challenges of Listed State-Owned Enterprises Around the World: National Experiences and a Framework for Reform. 50 *Cornell International Law Journal* 474.

Organisation for Economic Co-operation and Development (OECD). 2015. *Guidelines on Corporate Governance of State-Owned Enterprises*, 2015 edition.

Shareholder Empowerment Service. 2018. *Listed PSUs - Governance Gaps.*

Sobhan, F. and W. Wendy Werner (eds.). 2003. *A Comparative Analysis of Corporate Governance in South Asia: Charting a Roadmap for Bangladesh.* Bangladesh Enterprise Institute.

UK Government Investments Limited (UKGI). 2018. *Framework Document.*

UKGI. 2019. *Annual Report and Accounts 2018–2019.*

# 4 COMPLIANCE AND ANTI-MONEY LAUNDERING

## Introduction

In the "waterfall" of risk, regulation, and finally compliance, compliance serves as a key function to translate the understanding of risk into effective risk mitigation strategies on a firm level. While compliance is often seen by organizations and boards as necessary, but does not add value, it is key in helping to reduce risk in complex systems. Reducing risk is a very effective, and underappreciated, way of creating value in organizations. Effective compliance systems are also often the only way to be able to run complex operations. The standard example are modern aircrafts, which pilots can only control—and without almost any error—by following a rigorous regime of trained routines, supported by adequate checklists (compliance). In fact, it was the introduction of the checklist / compliance function that allowed the significant reduction of fatalities in the operation of jetliners.

Most organizations have not fully understood the value of compliance, and so treat it as a box-ticking exercise which, by definition, will not add value. It does not address the specific risk in an organization, but on the downside will create a lot of costs. People value security, and box-ticking provides them with the perceived security. It is also easy. Collectively, on organizational level, it will, however, be counterproductive as it will not help to reduce the risk while increasing costs.

Compliance comes essentially in two forms. First, the compliance of nonregulated firms mainly concerned with ensuring the compliance with laws and regulations, competition policy, and tax, among others. Tax governance has grown to be a topic in its own right. Other issues are legitimate stakeholder claims for example of workers and/or creditors, all of which are better handled internally than externally (e.g., in courts). Second, in regulated industries such as banking and finance, pharmaceuticals, or aerospace, society reserves the right to write much more numerous and intrusive regulations, and to closely monitor compliance with these regulations through dedicated enforcement agencies/bureaucracies. The state allows itself this quite considerable market intervention as any substantial error carries extensive negative externalities (costs) for society. But this is not necessarily bad, if firms understand that the rules are just a "codification" of known risk mitigation strategies. And once firms try to comply with the rules in a way that helps them to reduce their inherent risks as a company or their respective industries (and not mechanically), it will indeed help to create value for the organization.

Compliance takes many forms, from economic control or internal auditing to "corruption squads" checking the practices of foreign subsidiaries. Another form is "whistleblowing" where evidence is supplied by internal informants, who can report anonymously to a mailbox monitored not by company officers, but by a board member or a regulator.

The governance of the compliance function itself is subject to the same trade-offs that you find elsewhere in corporate governance. If compliance officers are part of a functional organization—for example, finance, accounting, or production—the risk is that they will end up trying to please their bosses and certify that their own functions are fully compliant. If, on the other hand, they are isolated and answer only to the top level of the organization—ultimately, to the board—the risk is that they will be insufficiently informed about what is going on and will make demands that are impractical. Since compliance officers are presumably no less self-serving than others, the compliance function can grow to enormous proportions. The sensible choice is likely to try to strike a balance that is in line with the risk preference of the board, and hence the firm.

## Governance, Risk, and Compliance

In practice, compliance is often merged with corporate governance, risk management, and IT compliance—collectively referred to as governance, risk, and compliance. From the viewpoint of the board, both compliance and risk management enforce limits and accountability in the organization in order to ensure that business is conducted in accordance with its rules, regulations, and policies. This also applies to IT which constitutes substantial operational risk. Moreover, it is hoped that better IT systems and improved administrative procedures will make it possible to get an overview over the many rules and procedures involved, and produce much better data on which the decisions are based. Ideally, this will then also result in the automation of tasks, so that the compliance staff can focus on the important cases, and not get bogged down with administrative tasks.

Practically, the enforcement is organized in a three-tier system, or three lines of defense (LOD). While the concept is discussed in detail in this study, it is important to understand that in an ideal world most decisions are done by frontline staff as part of their everyday routine. Additional checks are then added further up the hierarchy, which together form the three LOD:

   (i)    *First Line of Defense* by Operations/frontline staff—Execution.
   (ii)   *Second Line of Defense by Risk and Compliance*—Monitor and Control.
   (iii)  *Third Line of Defense* by (Internal) Auditor—Assurance.

## Compliance in Corporate Governance

The company secretary holds a key role in corporate governance compliance, in particular when it comes to board-related matters. The company secretary prepares the meeting and board papers, mails them out well ahead of time, sets the agenda, and then prepares the notes. The secretary also organizes a rigorous appointment process for new board members, organizes trainings (which in regulated industries can be compulsory), and, in general, makes sure that the board specific regulations are followed. The company secretary is supported by the legal Counsel, which then also helps prepare the Annual General Meeting, or if necessary, the Extraordinary General Meeting. In banks, the chief compliance officer has typically a seat on the management board, and sometimes a board seat.

## Compliance in Banks and Other Financial Industries

There is a substantial regulatory framework in place for banks, which is discussed here in detail as a model for all regulated industries as well as nonregulated industries. Banks serve as a good model for compliance as they belong to one of the most extensively regulated industries, and one with a long history of regulation. Banking supervision typically covers two broad concerns: banking stability and consumer protection. Each country, or monetary block, has an extensive resolution regime in place on how to deal with failing banks.

The supervisory authorities are interested in knowing the various risks banks are exposed to, such as financial and counterparty risk, reputational risk, embedded risk, data and consumer protection risks, and financial crime. Compliance should be a bread-and-butter business for banks, but surprisingly, it is not; or compliance is implemented "mechanically" (or un-intelligently), increasing banks' exposure to such risks.

### Anti-money Laundering Regime

The anti-money laundering (AML) regime is part of the financial crime compliance function. Similar to the concept of independent boards, it grew over the last 30 years from a niche concept to one that is at the forefront of policy making and regulation. Over the years, an extensive AML rule book has been developed, but unlike for independent boards, a lot of questions remain about the effectiveness of the various rules and procedures. AML is discussed in detail below.

### Compliance Is the Mirror of Risk

An extensive compliance function is required to avoid, and where not possible, mitigate risks. It is an important function given that these risks can potentially be very costly to industries and society, in general. Effective compliance begins with understanding the inherent risks in the business, and then establishing processes that are able to assess or measure (and manage) exposure to risks. If compliance is done mechanically, then it is missing the point and will be much less effective.

This report explores how risks emerge, how risks can be categorized, and how to deal with risks.

### Risks versus Issues

But what is risk? Risks are potential **future** problems. To evaluate risks, these three questions should be answered:

(i) What can go wrong?
(ii) Why will it happen (understand the cause)?
(iii) Why is this risk a problem?

The probability of an event occurring is assessed to help identify actions that will help solve or mitigate any potential risk. At this stage, a mandatory reporting process enables integrated reporting of risks from various sources (or departments), which allows the organization to assess the accepted level of risks and implement "control" measures.

Issues, on the other hand, are "hiccups" in the daily operations of the organizations that need to be resolved. Mitigation actions need to be identified and implemented to prevent these issues from happening again. Dealing with particular issues allows the organization to improve its understanding of risks, and how risks can be identified and mitigated.

### The Importance of Risk Management

Understanding where and how risks emerge is key to developing an effective and efficient compliance process. Emerging risks are hard to spot. With the use technology and other systems, organizations accumulate data, which would need to be managed (or interpreted) to arrive at valuable information that will help identify potential risks. Organizations often take into account previous experiences when making judgment on how to avoid or manage potential risks. The application of statistics, econometrics, and "machine learning" can help identify patterns and correlations in the data that can help generate early warning indicators or understand the underlying causes of risks. In general, understanding risks ahead of time can encourage or lead to innovation and other opportunities within the organization.

### Categorizing Risks

Risk is ubiquitous and can be overwhelming for any organization. A systematic approach to categorizing risk and then applying a methodical approach can help ease the burden. In general, risks can be categorized into different levels. Table 11 categorizes risks for banks into Level 1 and Level 2 lists. It is recommended that organizations likewise develop a similar taxonomy when identifying risks.

#### Table 11: Taxonomy of Risks

| Level 1 Risk | Level 2 Risk (Selected) |
|---|---|
| Credit Risk | • Counterparty risk<br>• Default risk<br>• Recovery risk<br>• Concentration risk<br>• Specialized lending portfolio risk<br>• Securitization risk<br>• Shadow banking risk |
| Market Risk | • Foreign exchange risk<br>• Interest rate risk<br>• Credit spread risk<br>• Equity risk<br>• Inflation risk<br>• Commodity risk<br>• Market liquidity risk |
| Liquidity Risk | • Wholesale funding risk<br>• Deposit risk<br>• Funding mismatch risk<br>• Intraday risk<br>• Off-balance sheet risk<br>• Marketable asset risk<br>• Non-marketable asset risk |
| Operational Risk | • Process risk<br>• IT Risk<br>• Reputational risk<br>• Conduct risk |

*continued on next page*

*Table 11 continued*

| Level 1 Risk | Level 2 Risk (Selected) |
|---|---|
| Compliance Risk | • Products and services<br>• Governance and internal processes<br>• Financial crime<br>• Market abuse<br>• Prudential reporting<br>• Security<br>• Data |
| Financial Model Risk | • Poor quantitative models |
| Insurance Risk | • Unexpected risk to due changes in assumptions, like:<br>  – longevity<br>  – volatility<br>  – climate |
| ESG Risk | • Environmental, social and governance (esg) risk<br>• Change in consumer expectation on esg<br>• De-carbonization of economy single-largest risk to firms and banks balance sheets |
| Business Model Risk | • Fintech<br>• Regtech |

Source: Adapted from CBS / Nordea / Plesner Course on Risk Management and Compliance.

**Figure: Risk Life Cycle**

Source: Authors.

It is helpful to have a good understanding of the risk life cycle and to organize the compliance process or processes accordingly. The process starts with a robust *planning* phase to have a good understanding what actually has to be changed (i.e., where to look). Then, *risk* that could negatively affect the aim (purpose) of the process (or of the organization, more generally) gets *identified.* . Then, *risk* is *assessed, quantified*, and *prioritized*. The aim is to assess what are the consequences of a threat occurring. Then, *risk mitigation* assesses whether to accept, try to mitigate, or to avoid risks. Organizations sometimes aim to avoid all risk, which is a very costly process, and can be highly inefficient. It can, indeed, be easier and cost-effective to accept certain risks, and then deal with the consequences if a negative event occurs. Robust *reporting and follow-up* must be an integral part of the process, not least to learn from the past and to keep senior management informed.

### Embedding Compliance in the Organization

By turning the abovementioned insights into action, an effective compliance process becomes not only robust, but also fast, efficient, and not cumbersome. Decision-making will be delegated to the person with the most information and most familiar about a particular case; in this case, the frontline staff is the first line of defense. As discussed, the three lines of defense (LOD) and their functions:

1. **First line of defense (1st LOD): Operations/frontline staff.**

    (i)    Operates within the agreed risk level, which is set by the board of directors. Accountable for identifying, mitigating, and reporting risk status. While it sounds trivial, they serve a very important task that needs considerable thought about adequate "on-the-ground" processes. It often involves redesigning the processes, with the positive spillover effect felt well beyond compliance as it allows for the modernization and updating of the defined tasks.

    (ii)   Promoting the right risk "culture" is another frontline task, which often goes hand-in-hand with redesigning the processes.

    (iii)  Works with the risk owners to ensure risks are identified, assessed, mitigated, monitored, and reported.

    (iv)   Training: Given the centrality of frontline staff for the success of the compliance process, the process re-engineering should be complemented with investment in training, so people really understand why they are doing what they are doing, and how to do it best. All this should pay for itself, as the costs of compliance should be offset by much higher efficiency, and better client service.
    *Purpose of 1st LOD: Execution.*

2. **Second line of defense (2nd LOD): Risk and Compliance.**

    This level is where much of the conceptual work happens, together with the oversight function of the frontline operations (1st LOD). It comprises the following functions:

    (i)    Designing the risk management frameworks.
    (ii)   Providing policies and guidelines.
    (iii)  Ensuring risk management oversight by independent monitoring and control of the 1st LOD.
    (iv)   *Purpose of 2nd LOD: Monitor and Control.*

3. **Third line of defense (3rd LOD): (Internal) Auditor**

This level is structurally removed from operations, and aims to provide independent oversight over the compliance function. It is part of the internal auditing process, but external auditors also provide oversight (and will need to justify their oversight and decisions once substantial problems emerge). It focuses on operational auditing of the internal control system.
*Purpose of 3rd LOD: Assurance.*

## Risk and Reporting Hierarchy

One big challenge in organizations is reporting up the hierarchy on risk, compliance, and governance. Risk-averse organizations often respond by over-reporting issues, which then over-burdens the board (as the highest point in the organization) with information. As a result, the board is unable to make timely and quality decisions.

Hence, clear guidelines (including examples) need to be written about the nature and scope of decision that each level is expected to make.

How does a typically risk hierarchy look like? Depending on the size of the firm it has about four to five levels, with the first, or bottom, being the first and second lines of defense. They report to an organizational risk committee, that then—depending on size—reports to a group risk committee. They report to, and ask counsel from, the executive management meeting. The final say is with the board, whose main task is to set the overall risk parameters for the firm. Common to most, if not all levels, will be an integrated risk reporting framework, which is followed to various degrees of detail across the company.

# On Compliance

Over the last 20 years, compliance in banks, in particular, and the financial industry, in general, became much more professionalized. Dedicated compliance functions are now required, with regulators also getting much more involved in monitoring compliance or related departments. In Europe, this only started in 2007 with MIFID I (*Markets in Financial Instruments Directive*) for securities traders, and after the financial crisis, more banks began establishing compliance departments. In 2014, MIFID II came to force, enhancing on the earlier proposals for the securities industry, and most certainly being informed by the experience of the financial crisis in 2008–2009. In the US, a similar process was started earlier in 2004 by the Committee of Sponsoring Organizations, but is—as typical for the US—a more market-based approach to regulation.

For this report, the main focus is compliance in banks, which gets typically extensively regulated by executive orders from banking regulators. Such orders are closely tied to being granted a banking license, and hence are well-enforced.

This report focuses on banks as they are by far the largest and most important industry in SAARC countries, and the operations of banks being central to the wealth of these nations. They also serve as a national "champion" for other and smaller regulated industries that might be able to adapt some of the compliance methods to their own requirements.

From a legal perspective, the main task of a compliance function is to monitor and assess the effectiveness of methods and procedures to identify and mitigate risks, and report the findings to the CEO, and the board of directors. The bank should make sure that: (i) compliance function is independent, (ii) there are no conflicts of interest, (iii) a compliance responsible person(s) is/are appointed, (iv) sufficient resources are allocated, (v) necessary competencies and knowledge to perform duties are in place, and (vi) there is access to all relevant information.

### Proportionality Is Key

It is important to note that a regulator applies the principle of proportionality when assessing the implementation of regulations. The regulator does not expect risk-free processes and operations, but one that focuses on identifying and solving the "big issues."

The banking supervisors typically focus on how the financial institution is organized (and in particular, the compliance function), instead of ensuring mechanical application of rules. Per industry experience, regulators allow considerable flexibility in interpretation of rules, very much in line with the argument above that good compliance should focus on the inherent risks in a (banking) operation, not just treating it as a mechanical box-ticking exercise.

### Digitalization and Workflow

Humans are best when making judgments, and machines are best in performing routine tasks. Unfortunately, in compliance, human brain power is more often wasted on routine tasks, while machines are likewise relegated to everyday routine tasks like e-mail and document processing.

As indicated, this report strongly encourages organizations to rethink processes and workflows, optimize, and then digitize. This is a task that ideally should not be outsourced, but rather driven from within the bank (technical consultants can help integrate or migrate workflow processes into IT systems). Improvements in efficiency will pay for the compliance function by itself. In addition, data collected systematically can then be used to employ intelligent statistics to improve the compliance function further, and deploy people more intelligently.

# Anti-money Laundering and Counter-Terror Finance

The global anti-money laundering (AML) standards were born out of a G7 initiative just over 30 years ago in 1989, which led to the creation of the Financial Action Task Force (FATF) on Money Laundering. It is based within the OECD headquarters in Paris. In 1995, an Asia-Pacific regional office called the FATF–Asia Secretariat was established as the precursor to the Asia/Pacific Group on Money Laundering (APG) that has been based in Sydney since 1997. Following the 9/11 attacks in 2001, the FATF remit was expanded to include counter-terror finance (CTF).

The FATF principles consist of 40 well established and formulated principles, which provide a sensible guideline on how to approach AML. Further, seven special provisions focus on CTF-related issues. Compliance with these principles is enforced through regular inspections by delegates from the member countries (peer review).

The FATF/APG principles helped to establish a common AML/CTF standard globally. The challenge lies in the uniform translation of these standards into commonly applied rules, in the lack of automation (as enforcement is expensive and cumbersome), and, more generally, efficient data sharing across various countries and institutions.

Before discussing current issues in detail, it is important to understand the different types of financial crime and money laundering, as it has very diverse actors and purposes, and so demands very different approaches.

First, there is attempt by organized crime groups to "clean" the proceeds of criminal activity. Often, these are proceeds from very serious crimes, with corresponding damaging impacts on society. Typical crimes in this category include drugs, human slavery, child exploitation, racketeering, fraud, and cybercrime. But society does not only suffer from the direct impact of the crime, but also indirectly once the proceeds get re-invested in society. This affects asset prices and market prices of goods as the illegal nature of the proceeds means firms financed by illegal money will be able to sustain losses or overpay for assets they purchase (e.g., houses and other real estate). This means that legitimate businesses are potentially driven out of the market.

Another category is the embezzlement of state funds, and the proceeds from tax evasion and corruption. This often involves very large amounts coming from states with weak institutions. Given that the amounts are substantial, these activities are highly profitable for intermediary financial institutions. More generally, as it involves another country, there is little incentive for institutions in intermediate countries to get involved. This applies to the Danske Bank case (potentially one of the largest-known cases of money laundering), where the Russian Central Bank was supposedly warned of the money laundering activities—a warning that was not heeded—possibly because it was deemed to be a case of simple tax evasion, and hence, a national issue.[124]

Finally, and in addition to money laundering, there is terror finance. Clearly a major concern globally, it is nevertheless practically undetectable by looking at the finance stream alone. The amounts involved are often trivial, with the proceeds used to rent apartments, cars, or purchase common household items. Unless it is related to organized crime, terror-related issues are best tackled through intelligence operations by the police, and not by the banking sector.

## Process

Detection of illicit payments starts with banks that are required to know their counterparties (banking customers), a process that is generally known as *Know Your Customer* (KYC). Banks often see this as very cumbersome and treat it as a box-ticking exercise. But it serves as an excellent opportunity for banks to learn more about their customers, and understand about the products or services they require, in addition to making sure that funds are not from illicit or illegal sources.

The banks then monitor the payment process and are obliged to report suspicious transactions in a Suspicious Activity Report (SAR) or Suspicious Transaction Report (STR)[125] to the financial

---

[124]   E. Bjerregaard and T. Kirchmaier. 2019. *The Danske Bank Money Laundering Scandal: A Case Study*. 2 September https://ssrn.com/abstract=3446636.

[125]   Different countries have different naming habits, with some calling SAR and some STR.

investigation unit (FIU). The FIU is part of the national police service and given that policing is either local or regional, it is not uncommon that particular transaction reaches the local police force. The bank suspends the suspicious transaction until the FIU has made a decision, which means that in practice a decision will need to be made by the FIU within 24 to 48 hours whether or not to block a particular payment.[126]

The degree of tolerance for suspicious payments varies across banks. Large banks often have strict controls in place, and also have little tolerance for these payments, while smaller banks are weaker on both dimensions.

One dimension that is often forgotten is that organizations and individuals that are listed on the sanction lists in the US, Europe, or other countries like Australia, Canada, or Switzerland. Banks should not deal with those and face hefty fines if transactions from those in such lists are processed in their respective currencies. Hence, they are best avoided. There are many commercial tools available that double check names (e.g., free open-source web software called Point.Exposed).[127]

One issue is that police services in most countries typically understaff FIUs, as police are more concerned with actual crime than investigating money laundering. This is compounded by the fact that FIUs suffer from terribly high staff turnover, as banks themselves pirate their staff. Hence, FIUs are often the weak point in the process. There is a lot of room for improving the detection mechanism through better algorithms, and sharing of data and information across the various institutions.

Another issue is the different treatment of banking subsidiaries and branches. Subsidiaries are freestanding units that are capitalized independently and supervised by the host country. Branches, on the other hand, do not carry their own capital and are supervised by the country of origin. In the Danske Bank case, the Estonian operation was organized as a branch, and supervised out of Copenhagen. While this is a very convenient arrangement for the banks (as they do not have to provide equity for the branch), it is not without risk, as these branches are typically lightly supervised, and often operate in local language. To demonstrate such risk, before the last financial crisis, AIG Banque (a subsidiary of the former US Insurance giant) held its banking license in France, but was booking all its problematic derivate position in London, leading to the largest-ever single bailout of $180 billion. In the case of AML, the institutional setup is even more complicated, as policing/FIU is a sovereign function and by definition local, while the branches are supervised centrally by the home country.

In summary, there is quite an elaborate global payment system from illicit finance, catering to individuals and organizations on sanctions lists. But it should be considered that the current banking/financial system is not perfect, and not without reason being considered very cumbersome and expensive. There is also anecdotal evidence that AML schemes more often targets small (or local) players instead of large, multinational organized crime groups.

The struggle to contain these organized crime groups is not surprising, as they are very efficient "globalized" enterprises, with professional money laundering a central part of the business model. As with all successful organizations, they have learned to specialize, and are creative and agile; even providing services for each other.

---

[126]  Albeit the maximum period is defined by local law.
[127]  This website also lists people that were listed in the Panama papers.

### The Way Forward: Standardize, Integrate, and Automate

The way forward is to improve the quality and speed of decision-making through automating "pre-sorting" or detection of suspicious transactions and their sources. This can be done using sophisticated statistics and machine learning, or so-called "big data." It is humans that still make the final judgment, but guided by a more efficient process. The considered golden rule with automation is that humans always make the final decision.[128]

To allow statistics to work, data collection needs to be standardized, in particular involving KYC and SARs/STRs. It is important that banks collect the data in the same format so they can report uniformly to the authorities, and where possible share data within the industry. Transaction data—the remaining data dimension—is already sufficiently standardized by central banks and using SWIFT standards.

Once standardized, data sets can be integrated (typically at the FIU or the central bank, but sometimes also at a third-party entity) to run much more efficient regressions. Once a good empirical detection model is developed (and here a word of warning for off-the-shelf solutions), automation can be applied and transfer much of the ongoing detection work to a machine.

# National Legal Frameworks on the AML/CTF Regulation and Guidelines

The following sections briefly summarize the key points of the legal framework on the AML/CTF regulation and guidelines of Bangladesh, Nepal, Pakistan, and Sri Lanka.

### *Bangladesh*

### Bangladesh and FATF

Similar to Pakistan, Bangladesh is not a member of the FATF, but is a member of APG. However, it is important to take note that Bangladesh is a founding member of AGP since 1997. Bangladesh is also one of the countries that have ratified the United Nations (UN) Vienna Convention against Illicit Traffic in Narcotics Drugs and Psychotropic Substances 1998, and the UN Convention for the Suppression of the Financing of Terrorism 1999.

The last two reports regarding Bangladesh's AML/CTF initiatives were the APG Mutual Evaluation Report 2016 (MER 2016) and the Follow-up Report 2019 ( FR 2019). Overall, the FR 2019 held Bangladesh to have "made good progress in addressing the technical compliance deficiencies identified in its MER...."[129]

---

[128]   The simple reason being is that humans are much better than machines in making judgments, and that it would be too expensive for machines to be completely error-free.

[129]   Asia/Pacific Group on Money Laundering (APG). 2019. Mutual Evaluation of Bangladesh. 3rd Enhanced Follow-Up Report. p. 10. http://www.apgml.org/members-and-observers/members/member-documents.aspx?m=060e4260-2ffd-4403-8594-6e4e8dc4b218.

**Legislation regarding AML/CTF and State Institutions Empowered with Supervision**

Legislation/Regulations/Guidelines

*Money Laundering Prevention Act, 2012*

The primary legislative instrument in Bangladesh regarding AML/CTF is the Money Laundering Prevention Act, 2012 (MLPA 2012). Section 2(v) provides a rather extensive definition of money laundering:

(i)    "knowingly moving, converting, or transferring proceeds of crime or property involved in an offence for the following purposes:- (1) concealing or disguising the illicit nature, source, location, ownership or control of the proceeds of crime; or (2) assisting any person involved in the commission of the predicate offence to evade the legal consequences of such offence;

(ii)   smuggling money or property earned through legal or illegal means to a foreign country;

(iii)  knowingly transferring or remitting the proceeds of crime to a foreign country or remitting or bringing them into Bangladesh from a foreign country with the intention of hiding or disguising its illegal source; or

(iv)   concluding or attempting to conclude financial transactions in such a manner so as to reporting requirement under this Act may be avoided;

(v)    converting or moving or transferring property with the intention to instigate or assist for committing a predicate offence;

(vi)   acquiring, possessing or using any property, knowing that such property is the proceeds of a predicate offence;

(vii)  performing such activities so as to the illegal source of the proceeds of crime may be concealed or disguised;

(viii) participating in, associating with, conspiring, attempting, abetting, instigate or counsel to commit any offences mentioned above"

Sec. 2(z)(cc) provides a list of 28 offenses which are deemed as "predicate offenses." Interestingly, the last of these is *"any other offence declared as predicate offence by Bangladesh Bank, with the approval of the Government, by notification in the official Gazette, for the purpose of this Act."* What is interesting about this is that the power to declare any act as a predicate offense lies with Bangladesh Bank. Even though the approval of the government is required, this is a substantial power to be placed in the hands of the bank.

By way of Section 9 of the MLPA 2012, the power to investigate offenses under the MLPA rests with the Anti-Corruption Commission.[130] The MLPA also makes the offenses cognizable and non-bailable.[131] MLPA 2012, by Sec. 14, gives power for freezing or attaching any property involved in money laundering.

Sec. 23 of the MLPA places certain responsibilities upon the Bangladesh Bank, and Sec. 24 provides for the establishment of Bangladesh Financial Intelligence Unit (BFIU).

---

[130]  Established by the Anti-Corruption Commission 2004
[131]  Money Laundering Prevention Act, 2012, Sec. 11.

*Anti-Terrorism Act 2009*

Section 7 of the Anti-Terrorism Act 2009 expressly makes an offense of terror financing. Sec. 7(1) of the Anti-Terrorism Act 2009 states:

> "7(1) If any person or entity will-fully provides, receives, collects or makes arrangements for money, service or any other property, whether from legitimate or illegitimate source, by any means, directly or indirectly, with the intention that, in full or in part (a) it will be used to carry out terrorist activity; (b) it will be used for any purposes by terrorist person or entity or in the knowledge that they are to be used by terrorist person or entity; the said person or entity shall commit the offence of terrorist financing."

Sec. 15 of the Anti-Terrorism Act 2009 also grants powers to the Bangladesh Bank regarding terror financing.

Money laundering and terror financing are substantially less spread out across various laws and institutions than in other jurisdictions, such as Pakistan. This gives the entire regime a particular efficiency since this can reduce the information sharing time, and the amount of coordination required by the institutions.

## Institutions

There are two primary institutions in Bangladesh that deal with the issue of AML/CTF: Bangladesh Bank and Bangladesh Financial Intelligence Unit (BFIU).

The Bangladesh Bank is a corporate body that was established pursuant to the Bangladesh Bank Order, 1972. One of the key functions of the Bangladesh Bank is the prevention of money laundering. The bank has issued several guidelines regarding money laundering and terror financing. These guidelines are aimed, specifically, at various institutions: banking sector, financial institutions, NPO/NGO sector, insurance companies, etc.

The "BFIU has been entrusted with the responsibility of exchanging information related to ML & TF with its foreign counterparts. The main objective of BFIU is to establish an effective system for prevention of money laundering, combat financing of terrorism and proliferation of weapons of mass destruction and it has been bestowed with operational independence."[132]

MLPA 2012 has rendered the BFIU operationally independent. BFIU issues numerous circulars and guidelines regarding money laundering in order to regulate AML/CTF and keep stakeholders up-to-date with information regarding AML/CTF.

The operation and the initiatives of these two institutions seem to work well for Bangladesh as they have received approval in the reports published by APG regarding Bangladesh's compliance with FATF requirements.

---

[132] Basic Bank Limited. 2016. Anti-Money Laundering (AML) and Combating of Terror Financing (CTF) Policy (1st Revision). https://www.basicbanklimited.com/files/AML_and_CFT_Policy_of_BASIC_Bank_2016.pdf, p. 22.

What do the reports say regarding the legal framework/ compliance with FATF recommendations?

*Mutual Evaluation Report 2016*

MER 2016, which evaluated Bangladesh's AML/CTF initiatives, produced, *inter alia,* the following conclusions:

(i)     Overall, Bangladesh has made significant progress since 2009.

(ii)    Competent authorities have a reasonable understanding of the money laundering and terror financing risks. Interagency work to assess terror financing risks show strength, but need more work.

(iii)   The National Coordination Committee was lauded for being effective. Sufficient functioning policy coordination structures were made, however, at an operational level; higher level of coordination and cooperation was required.

(iv)    Corruption-based money laundering still remains an unmitigated area.

(v)     The Financial Intelligence Unit (FIU) was seen to demonstrate strength. However, improvement to reporting to the Financial Intelligence Unit was required.

(vi)    Law enforcement agencies needed to prioritize tracing, restraint, and confiscation of proceeds. The powers of FIU and the National Board of Revenue related to this added to effectiveness.

(vii)   Courts and Attorney General's office were seriously under-resourced.

(viii)  Level of investigation and prosecution of terror financing matters added to effectiveness. However, issue of financing of foreign "fighters" still remained an issue.

(ix)    AML measures regarding NPOs went beyond the obligations in the FATF standards; however, the oversight and supervision does not adequately target terror financing risk.

(x)     Frequency, scope, and intensity of on-site inspections of commercial banks and nonbank financial institutions were generally sufficient; however, there were inadequate resources available to undertake comprehensive supervision across all sectors.

(xi)    Measures to ensure transparency and prevent misuse of legal persons and arrangements were not well established or implemented.

(xii)   Strong commitment to international cooperation and its open and responsive approach to fulfill requests received from foreign partners was demonstrated. The overall level and focus of requests for international cooperation by law enforcement agencies, customs, and prosecutors was not in keeping with the risk profile.

*Follow-up Report 2019*

Bangladesh requested the re-rating of five recommendations, all of which were rated PC (partial compliance). Table 12 shows details, as well as the conclusions, regarding the recommendations.

## Table 12: Recommendations and Conclusions

| Recommendation No. | Details of Recommendation | Rating | Reasoning Provided |
|---|---|---|---|
| Recommendation No. 9 | Financial Institution Secrecy Laws–Bangladesh had not issued exemptions for financial institutions to undertake information sharing | Largely compliant | Bangladesh issued Money Laundering Prevention Rules (MLPR), 2019 and Circular No. 22, dated 31 January 2019, which addressed the deficiencies to a large extent. Although both the documents do not specify what is meant by information on reliance of third-parties, thus minor deficiencies remain. |
| Recommendation No. 16 | Wire Transfers–Deficiencies that were noted included no requirement for financial institutions to collect a unique transaction number in the absence of an account number; inter-bank wire transfers were exempt from the requirement to collect transfer information and there is no express prohibition on ordering banks executing wire transfers if requirements for wire transfers are not met. | Compliant | Bangladesh Financial Intelligence Unit (BFIU) Circular No. 21, dated 30 January 2019, was issued which corrected all the deficiencies present in the system. |
| Recommendation No. 18 | Internal Control and Foreign Branches and Subsidiaries – There was no specific requirements for financial institutions to implement group-wide anti-money laundering and counter-terror finance (AML/CTF) policies and procedures, and no requirements on foreign branches or subsidiary branches of insurance companies, capital markets intermediaries, and money changes. | Compliant | Bangladesh issued MLPR 2019, which generally requires financial institutions to implement, where applicable, group-wide AML/CFT program and policies. These policies should include information sharing provisions and procedures. BFIU Circular No. 23, dated 31 January 2019, also provides detail on AML/CFT program and policies for the financial group and information sharing among the institutions under the group. |

*continued on next page*

*Table 12  continued*

| Recommendation No. | Details of Recommendation | Rating | Reasoning Provided |
|---|---|---|---|
| Recommendation No. 26 | Regulation and Supervision of Financial Institutions—Certain deficiencies were noted: fit and proper checks for financial institutions do not extend to beneficial ownership, limited measures in place to prevent criminals from holding a license or managing a financial institution, and that on-site supervision was not expanded beyond banks. Also, here was no formal mechanism in place for supervisors to update assessment of sector money laundering/terror financing risks where there are major events/changes to a financial institution or sector, and no formal mechanism to evaluate shareholders/senior management for stock dealers, brokers, and authorized representatives. | Largely compliant | Through the amended MLPR 2019 and particularly section 32(1), Bangladesh requires all regulatory authorities to implement a market entry control mechanism while issuing a license, granting registration, or approving business activities which includes steps to be taken to prevent criminals or their associates being the owners, directors, managers, or beneficial owners of Reporting Organizations (ROs). |
| Recommendation No. 34 | Guidance and Feedback – Bangladesh had not issued sufficient guidance on terror financing risks, and had not produced guidance covering the most pressing elements of money laundering risk, including those arising from domestic politically exposed persons (PEPs), corruption (e.g., state-owned commercial banks, public sector procurement), fraud, smuggling, and the capital market. | Largely compliant | BFIU issued guidance to ROs on terror financing and proliferation financing, and has therefore addressed this deficiency. However, there is still no guidance provided on corruption, fraud risks, smuggling risks, and risks associated with capital market and state-owned commercial banks. BFIU issued guidelines/guidance notes on 27 January 2019 on PEPs, reporting suspicious transactions, and beneficial ownership for ROs. BFIU provided feedback to ROs in 2018, including feedback to financial institutions, insurance companies, and money changers. In addition, BFIU provided further guidance in feedback sessions relating to Suspicious Activity Reports and Currency Transaction Reports . The review team found that Bangladesh has addressed the deficiencies to a large extent, but that some deficiencies remain. |

Source: Authors.

## *Nepal*

### Nepal and FATF

Nepal is not a member of the FATF. However, it has been a member of the APG since June 2002. The last report on Nepal's money laundering and terror financing initiatives was published in July 2011. Similar to other countries, Nepal has also created a Financial Information Unit which operates as Nepal's financial intelligence unit (FIU).

### Legislation regarding AML/CTF and State Institutions Empowered with Supervision

*Legislation/Regulations/Guidelines*

The primary legislation in Nepal for AML/CTF is the Asset (Money) Laundering Act (AMLA) 2008. The AMLA makes provisions which make money laundering and terror financing a crime and provide for punishment for the offenders. Section 3 of the AMLA provides:

(i)   "Nobody shall launder or cause to launder assets."
(ii)  "Any one committing acts pursuant to sub-section (1) shall be deemed to have committed offence as per this Act."

Sec. 4 provides an explanation as to what "shall launder or cause to launder assets" is:

"4: Assets shall be supposed to have laundered in case anyone, directly or indirectly, earns from tax evasion or terrorist activities or invests in such activities or acquires, holds, possesses or utilizes assets by committing any or all offences stipulated as follows and in case assets acquired, held or accumulated from investment of such assets is possessed, held or used, utilized or consumed or committed any other act so as to present such assets as legally acquired or earned assets or conceals sources of origin of such assets or assists any one to transform, conceal or transfer such assets with an objective of avoiding legal actions to the person having such assets:- (a) Offences under the prevailing arms and ammunitions laws, (b) Offences under the prevailing foreign exchange regulation laws, (c) Offences of murder, theft, cheating, forgery documents, counterfeiting, kidnap or abduction under the concerned prevailing laws, (d) Offences under the prevailing drug addiction control laws, (e) Offences under the prevailing national park and wild animals conservation laws, (f) Offences under the prevailing human trafficking and taking of hostages control laws, (g) Offences under the prevailing cooperatives laws, (h) Offences under the prevailing forest laws, (i) Offences under the prevailing corruption control laws, (j) Offences under the prevailing bank and financial institution laws, (k) Offences under the prevailing banking crime and punishment laws, (l) Offences under the prevailing ancient monuments conversation laws, (m) Other offences that Government of Nepal prescribes by publishing in the Nepal Gazette."

The punishment for an offense under Sec. 3 is provided in Sec. 30. The punishment includes a fine of the amount of laundered assets, and imprisonment from 1 to 4 years (which seems low given the gravity of the offense and comparing this with punishment in other jurisdictions).

The AMLA also contains provisions for the freezing of assets related to money laundering and terror financing, and the power rests with the investigative authority.[133] Sec. 19 provides for the suspension of transactions or accounts related to money laundering.

Pertinently, terror financing has not been made a separate offense.

Various departments including the FIU and the Department of Cooperatives have issued guidelines and directives regarding AML/CTF.[134]

### Institutions

There are a number of bodies and institutions in Nepal responsible for AML/CTF.

The Financial Information Unit was created by Sec. 9 of the Asset (Money) Laundering Act 2008, which provides:

(i)   "There shall be a Financial Information Unit in Rastra Bank for collection and analysis of information relating to assets laundering."

(ii)  "The Governor of Rastra Bank shall appoint the chief of the Financial Information Unit from among the first class officers, at the least, of Rastra Bank."

(iii) "The Office of the Financial Information Unit shall be placed in Rastra Bank and the Rastra Bank shall manage the staffs required for it."

The FIU is an operationally independent unit placed within the Nepal Rastra Bank (NRB). Its functions are provided in Sec. 10 of the AMLA 2008 and include, *inter alia*, obtaining details of suspicious transactions and evaluating the information attained.

AMLA 2008 also creates a Coordination Committee, which comprises of the director of the FIU; the secretaries of the ministries of finance, law, home, and foreign affairs; and the deputy governor of the NRB.[135] The aim of this committee is to increase coordination between different government departments regarding AML/CTF. A collective committee of the head of various departments can allow for increased efficiency.

Sec. 11 of the AMLA creates the Asset Laundering Prevention Department, which is tasked with the investigation of the offenses under the AMLA.

*What do the reports say regarding the legal framework/ compliance with FATF recommendations?*

*Mutual Evaluation Report 2011*

In July 2011, a Mutual Evaluation Report (MER 2011) was published, which evaluated Nepal's initiatives regarding money laundering and terror financing. The key findings of MER 2011 are as follows:

- The main offenses in Nepal which create money laundering and terror financing risks are drug trafficking, human trafficking, arms trafficking, corruption, counterfeit currency, tax evasion, and gold smuggling.

---

133   Asset (Money) Laundering Act (AMLA) 2008, Sec. 18.
134   Nepal Rastra Bank https://www.nrb.org.np/fiu/index.php.
135   Asset (Money) Laundering Act (AMLA) 2008, Sec. 8.

- There are significant deficiencies in Nepal's AML legislation. The range of predicate offenses is not too wide enough to comply with FATF standards. Ancillary offenses do not extend to conspiracy and possibly do not cover aiding of the commission of a predicate offense.

- Even though terror financing is included in the definition of money laundering in the legislation, terror financing is not criminalized separately.

- The legislation which provides the mechanism for freeing the assets of terrorists listed under UN Security Council Regulation 1267 is a subordinate legislation, and thus is not binding.

- Nepal's FIU is a departmental unit within the Nepal Rastra Bank (central bank). FIU lacks sufficient administrative basis for its continuing operations. It also lacks sufficient skill and resources.

- Financial institutions, as well as some nonfinancial institutions (including casinos), are required to file STRs and threshold transaction reports, but significant deficiencies in the money laundering offense and the lack of a terror financing offense narrows the scope of reporting.

- The instruments imposing requirements on financial and nonfinancial institutions to adopt AML/CTF preventive measures are not enforceable, and there are gaps in the scope of institutions included.

- Customer identification and verification is a weakness in Nepal's preventive measures. The measures which purport to impose identification requirements for nonbanks are not binding.

- Nepal does not have a mutual legal assistance law.

## *Pakistan*

### Pakistan and FATF

Pakistan became a member of the APG in May 2000. The latest report regarding AML/CTF measures in relation to FATF was published in October of 2019.

In June 2018, Pakistan was placed in the "grey" list of the FATF.[136]

### Legislation regarding AML/CTF and State Institutions Empowered with Supervision

Legislation/Regulations/Guidelines

#### *Anti-Money Laundering Act 2010*

The Anti-Money Laundering Act 2010 (AMLA) repealed and replaced the Anti-Money Laundering Ordinance 2007 (AMLO. The scope of AMLO was limited to account transactions and suspicious transaction reports (SRO) were restricted to only banking accounts. The offense of money laundering was made non-cognizable and a small number of predicate offences were included in the schedule of the AMLO (footnote 136).

AMLA was enacted with a broader scope. Section 3 of the AMLA defines money laundering. The definition is extensive. Sec. 3 states:

---

[136] I. Ali. Anti-Money Laundering Act 2010: A Critical Analysis. https://sahsol.lums.edu.pk/law-journal/anti-money-laundering-act-2010-critical-analysis.

"A person shall be guilty of offence of money laundering, if the person:

a. Acquires, converts, possesses, uses or transfers property, knowing or having reason to believe that such property is proceeds of crime;

b. Conceals or disguises the true nature, origin, location, disposition, movement or ownership of property, knowing or having reason to believe that such property is proceeds of crime;

c. holds or possesses on behalf of any other person any property knowing or having reason to believe that such property is proceeds of crime; or

d. Participates in, associates, conspires to commit, attempts to commit, aids, abets, facilitates, or counsels the commission of the acts specified in clauses (a), (b), and (c)."

Sec. 4 provides that the punishment of the offense contained in Sec. 3 shall be imprisonment of 1–10 years and a fine of up to PRs1 million, as well as liability for forfeiture of the property involved in the money laundering. It further provides that in the case of a company, the fine can extend to up to PRs5 million rupees and every director, employee, or officer of the company involved shall be punished under this section.

Sections 9, 10, and 11 provide for the attachment and forfeiture of property relating to money laundering, or the source of which is a crime.

AMLA also contains provisions for the creation of a National Executive Committee to combat money laundering[137] and the Financial Monitoring Unit.[138]

### Anti-Terrorism Act 1997

Section 11K of the Anti-Terrorism Act 1997 makes it an offense for anyone to launder money intentionally, for any person or organization labeled as terrorist and/or terrorist organization by the federal government. The punishment for this offense is imprisonment of a term 5–10 years.[139]

Sec. 110 of the Anti-Terrorism Act 1997 allows for the seizure, freeze, and detention of any property or money owned by any person or organization labeled as terrorist and/or terrorist organization by the federal government.

### Control of Narcotics Substances Act 1997

Section 37 of the Control of Narcotics Substances Act 1997 allows for the freezing of assets of any person if the court is satisfied that the person owning the asset has committed a crime under the act. Sec. 67 directs banks and financial institutions to pay attention to unusual patterns of transactions and report all transactions that are under suspicion of being related to narcotics. Failure to report such information can result in imprisonment of up to 3 years.

### Regulations Promulgated by the State Bank of Pakistan

There are three main regulations that have been promulgated by the State Bank of Pakistan (SBP): AML/CTF Regulations for Banks and Domestic Financial Institutions, AML/CTF Guidelines on Risk

---

[137]  Anti-Money Laundering Act 2010, Sec. 5.

[138]  Anti-Money Laundering Act 2010, Sec. 6.

[139]  Anti-Terrorism Act 1997, Sec. 11N.

Based Approach for Banks and DFIs, and Guidance on Compliance of Government of Pakistan's Notification issued under United Nations Security Council (UNSC) Regulations.[140]

### Guidelines and Regulations by the Securities and Exchange Commission of Pakistan

The Securities and Exchange Commission of Pakistan (SECP) has also released various guidelines, regulations, circulars, and yearly FAQs for guidance of the corporate sector of Pakistan in relation to AML/ CFT.[141]

## Institutions

There are two types of institutions/bodies involved with AML/CTF in Pakistan: regulatory bodies and investigative and prosecution bodies.

### Regulatory

There are three primary regulatory bodies in Pakistan in regard to AML/CTF: the State Bank of Pakistan (SBP),[142] which is charged with the regulation of the monetary and credit system of Pakistan; the Securities and Exchange Commission of Pakistan (SECP), which is charged with the regulation of the corporate sector of Pakistan; and the Financial Monitoring Unit (FMU),[143] which is housed in the SBP but has independent decision-making authority on day-to-day matters coming within its areas of responsibility."[144] The powers and functions of the FMU are listed in Sec. 6(4) AMLA and include, *inter alia*, receiving Suspicious Transaction Reports and CTRs from financial institutions, analyzing them, creating corresponding databases, cooperating with financial intelligence units in other countries, making annual recommendations to the National Executive Committee, and framing regulations with the SBP and the SECP.

Since each of these bodies is a separate, independent entity, they exercise sufficient and unhindered, authority regarding AML/CTF from a regulatory perspective.

### Investigative and Prosecution Bodies

Section 2(j) of the AMLA provides the definition of investigating or prosecuting agency. The definition states that:

> "investigating or prosecuting agency" means the National Accountability Bureau (NAB), Federal Investigation Agency (FIA), Anti-Narcotics Force (ANF), or any other law enforcement agency as may be notified by the Federal Government for the investigation or prosecution of a predicate offence."[145]

---

[140]    Available at: http://www.sbp.org.pk/l_frame/aml.htm.

[141]    Available at: https://www.secp.gov.pk/aml-cft-2/aml-cft-laws/aml-cft-circulars/.

[142]    Created by Sec 3 of the State Bank of Pakistan Act, 1956.

[143]    Created by Sec 6 of the AMLA.

[144]    Anti-Money Laundering Act 2010, Sec. 6(2).

[145]    A predicate offense, per Sec. 2(s) AMLA, is an offense specified in the Schedule to the Act.

Apart from NAB, FIA, and ANF, the Directorate General (Intelligence and Investigation Inland Revenue) Federal Board of Revenue was also included as an investigating or prosecuting agency pursuant to a notification by Ministry of Finance and Revenue dated 24 August 2010.[146]

Although these agencies are well-equipped, they are not successful in stopping money laundering. The reason being that each agency has a different mandate, operative jurisdiction, and powers; thus, there is a lack of a centralized authority for the investigation or prosecution of money laundering/terror financing offenses (especially the offense of money laundering as provided in the AMLA).

The NAB has no power to investigate and prosecute cases concerning terrorist financing and this is because the schedule of the ordinance[147] fails to include it as an offense.[148] FIA cannot operate at the provincial level and cannot deal with the offenses committed solely by private persons.[149] Further, offenses under the Anti-Terrorism Act 1997 are included in the schedule of the FIA Act 1974,[150] but the federal agency can only deal with those terrorist financing cases, which have an inter-provincial scope or are assigned by the federal government.[151] The powers of the ANF are only to the extent of the offenses under the Control of Narcotics Substances Act, 1997. Finally, the Federal Board of Revenue has the power to investigate and prosecute the cases under AMLA wherever earnings of crimes are accumulated under the offenses committed under the Customs Act, 1969.[152]

Perhaps one of the major problems regarding AML/CTF in Pakistan is that there is a lack of a single investigative/prosecution body. Rather, the powers are spread out, and thus AML/CTF tasks become more difficult to complete and problems more difficult to tackle.

What do the reports say regarding the legal framework/ compliance with FATF recommendations?

In October 2019, the AGP published a report titled "Anti-money laundering and counter-terrorist financing measures" in relation to Pakistan. The report deemed that measures taken by Pakistan relating to AML/CTF were not sufficient. The key findings of the report are summarized as follows:

(i)   Authorities and corporations require more understanding of the risks of money laundering and terror financing. Also, Pakistan's multiagency approach toward the implementation of AML/CTF needs a more coordinated risk-based approach.

(ii)  There is a greater need of spontaneous information sharing between FMU and provincial counter-terrorism departments.

(iii) Pakistan's law enforcement authorities' efforts to address money laundering are not consistent with its risks.

(iv)  Value of confiscated funds is not proportional to the risk.

(v)   A higher rate of terror financing convictions is required in provinces other than Punjab.

---

[146]  I. Ali. Anti-Money Laundering Act 2010: A Critical Analysis available at https://sahsol.lums.edu.pk/law-journal/anti-money-laundering-act-2010-critical-analysis.

[147]  The National Accountability Ordinance under which the NAB was established and empowered.

[148]  Footnote 146.

[149]  Footnote 146.

[150]  The act which established and empowers the FIA.

[151]  Footnote 146.

[152]  Footnote 146.

(vi)  The nonbanking sector and designated nonfinancial businesses and professions (DNFBPs) are not conducting sufficient checks and screening to identify people acting on behalf of, or at the direction of, a designated entity or person, and have not frozen any funds.

(vii) SBP and SECP need to take more focused action on terror financing risks and proliferation financing.

(viii) SBP does not have sufficient understanding regarding money laundering and terror financing in its own sector. However, it is making improvements. SECP has limited understanding of the money laundering and terror financing risks.

(ix)  Inadequate measures to address risks imposed by trusts, including foreign trusts.

(x)  Inadequate number of money laundering-related and terror financing-related mutual legal assistance requests by Pakistan when compared to its risks.

## Sri Lanka

### Sri Lanka and FATF

Like Bangladesh, Sri Lanka is also a founding member of the APG (thus, has been a member since 1997), but is not a member of the FATF. Sri Lanka has had difficulties in the past with terrorism from the Liberation Tigers of Tamil Eelam. Steps taken by Sri Lanka regarding terror financing and terrorism have been rather robust. The reports regarding Sri Lanka indicate that initiatives against terror financing in Sri Lanka are better and more potent in their operation than those for money laundering. However, in 2019, the rating for Sri Lanka regarding certain recommendations of the FATF was re-evaluated, upon request, and was improved.

### Legislation regarding AML/CTF and State Institutions Empowered with Supervision

#### Legislation/Regulations/Guidelines

Sri Lanka's AML/CTF legislative regime comprises of three pieces of legislation.

#### Financial Transactions Reporting Act, No. 6 of 2006

The Financial Transactions Reporting Act (FTRA) aims to grant powers to the Financial Intelligence Unit (FIU) and elaborate its functions. Further, FTRA created provisions which obligated financial institutions to report transactions to the FIU which, it is suspected, are connected with money laundering and terror financing. Section 15 of the FTRA provides for the functions of the FIU, which include receiving reports by financial institutions, analyzing those reports, compelling the provision of the information, etc. Sec. 2(3) also empowers the FIU to issue rules to financial institutions. Sec. 4 requires financial institutions to maintain records of transactions and correspondences in relation thereto. Sec. 7 obligates institutions to report any transactions that they suspect are connected with terrorism or money laundering to the FIU.

#### Prevention of Money Laundering Act, No. 5 of 2006

The Prevention of Money Laundering Act (PMLA) creates provisions making money laundering, aiding or abetting money laundering, or any action in connection thereto, an offense. The offense is contained in Section 3 of the PMLA. Sec 3 provides:

(i)    Any person, who—

(a) engages directly or indirectly in any transaction in relation to any property which is derived or realised, directly or indirectly, from any unlawful activity or from the proceeds of any unlawful activity;

(b) receives, possesses, conceals, disposes of, or brings into Sri Lanka, transfers out of Sri Lanka, or invests in Sri Lanka, any property which is derived or realised, directly or indirectly, from any unlawful activity or from the proceeds of any unlawful activity,

*knowing or having reason to believe that such property is derived or realised, directly or indirectly from any unlawful activity or from the proceeds of any unlawful activity, shall be guilty of the offence of money laundering and shall on conviction after trial before the High Court be liable to a fine not less than the value of the property in respect of which the offence is committed and not more than three times the value of the property in respect of which the offence is committed or to rigorous imprisonment for a period of not less than five years and not exceeding twenty years, or to both such fine and imprisonment. The assets of any person found guilty of the offence of money laundering under this section shall be liable to forfeiture in terms of Part II, of this Act."*

Part II of the PMLA, entitled "Freezing and Forfeiture of Assets in Relation to the Offence of Money Laundering," contains provisions regarding the forfeiture of the assets of people in relation to money laundering.

### Convention of the Suppression of Terrorist Financing Act, No. 25 of 2005

The Convention of the Suppression of Terrorist Financing Act was enacted by Sri Lanka to give effect to the country's obligations under the International Convention on the Suppression of Terrorist Financing, which was adopted by the General Assembly of the United Nations in 1999.[153] The act is specifically aimed toward acts of terrorism and terror financing. It creates provisions making terror financing, and aiding or abetting terror financing, a crime, and provisions for the forfeiture of any property in relation thereto.

### Rules, Circulars, and Guidelines by the Financial Intelligence Unit

The FIU has been given the power under Section 2 of the FTRA to make rules. Using this power, the FIU has promulgated numerous rules aimed at specific financial institutions and for costumer due diligence.[154] The FIU has also been promulgating circulars and guidelines with the aim of increasing an understanding of the institutions and people regarding AML/CTF.[155]

## Institutions

### Financial Intelligence Unit

The FIU of Sri Lanka is the main body tasked with combating money laundering and terror financing. Its responsibilities include the strengthening of the AML/CTF regime, and upgrading the compliance level of Sri Lanka with international standards for AML/CTF. The FIU is the central repository of the reports and information regarding AML/CTF by financial institutions. The functions related to AML/CTF are vested solely in this institution, allowing for greater consistency and efficiency. FIU has been successful in improving compliance with the FATF requirements by Sri Lanka and this point is reflected in the Follow-up Report, 2019.

---

[153]   Preamble to the Convention of the Suppression of Terrorist Financing Act.

[154]   These rules are available at http://www.fiusrilanka.gov.lk/rules_directions.html.

[155]   These are available at the Financial Intelligent Unit of Sri Lanka website: http://www.fiusrilanka.gov.lk/circulars_guidelines.html.

*Other Bodies*

Other institutions related to AML/CTF are the Sri Lanka Police, which is tasked with the investigation and general policing of money laundering and terror financing, and the Central Bank of Sri Lanka, which is tasked with the general supervision of the entire monetary system of Sri Lanka.

*What do the reports say regarding the legal framework/ compliance with FATF recommendations?*

The last mutual evaluation report on Sri Lanka was published in the year 2015, and since then no additional report has been published. However, in October 2019, a follow-up report was published by AGP regarding the initiatives taken by Sri Lanka to combat terror financing and money laundering, wherein ratings of Sri Lanka for certain FATF recommendations were re-evaluated.

*Mutual Evaluation Report 2015*

The key findings of the Mutual Evaluation Report 2015 (MER 2015) for Sri Lanka were as follows:

- Sri Lanka has an "acute" understanding of its risks regarding terror financing and has a reasonable understanding of its risks regarding money laundering. However, its understanding regarding money laundering has not been translated well into a national AML strategy.
- Sri Lanka has not adopted a risk-based approach to AML/CTF.
- Sri Lanka's use of financial intelligence regarding terror financing and money laundering does not extend to the full range of potentially relevant information. The FIU is not using financial information or other available information to undertake strategic analysis.
- Sri Lanka possesses the foundation of an effective AML system, but the conviction rate and prosecution rate are too low, which reflect the jurisdiction's lack of capacity.
- Sri Lanka's success in CFT is a result of high-level government commitment, and multi-pronged and well-coordinated efforts among agencies. It also has a clear and high-level national policy focus on deterring terrorist activities especially through confiscating the assets of terrorists.
- The Prevention of Terrorism Act 1979 has been used as a legislative tool to successfully deprive terrorist organizations of funds and property. However, Sri Lanka has been less effective in prosecuting terror financing cases especially with foreign elements given the challenges with international cooperation to obtain evidence to prosecute terrorist financiers.
- Sri Lanka has not yet dealt with proliferation financing.
- Sri Lanka has not successfully assessed the money laundering and terror financing risk with respect to the use of legal persons and arrangements.
- Significant gaps exist in regard to rules pertaining to requirements in a number of key areas such as costumer due diligence, politically exposed persons, high-risk countries, internal controls, correspondent banking, wire transfer, and money value transfer service.
- The level of understanding of financial institutions regarding money laundering and terror financing varies across sectors and institutions. There is a need for stronger application of a risk-based approach.
- Apart from banks, the relevant supervisory authorities lack clear powers to prevent criminals from participating as beneficial owners in financial institutions and DNFBPs.
- The Financial Intelligence Unit is under-resourced.
- The central authority does not adequately maintain and monitor the status and timeliness of requests made and obtained.

*Follow-up Report 2019*

Upon Sri Lanka's request to re-evaluate its status in regard to six recommendations, the Follow-up Report 2019 (FR 2019) was published. The details of the recommendations and the conclusions of the FR Report are reproduced in the Table 13.

**Table 13: Recommendations and Conclusions of the Follow-Up Report 2019**

| Recommendation No. | Details of Recommendation | Rating Given | Reasoning Provided |
|---|---|---|---|
| No. 7 | Targeted financial sanctions related to proliferation (initial rating: Noncompliant)–Sri Lanka had taken no formal effect to proliferation financing sanctions. | Largely Compliant | Sri Lanka has taken numerous legislative and implementation steps for targeted financial sanctions for proliferation financing. A wide number of civil, administrative, and criminal sanctions are available for persons, financial institutions, and designated nonfinancial businesses and professions (DNFBPs) should they not comply with the relevant regulations. |
| No. 25 | Transparency and beneficial ownership of legal arrangements (initial rating: Noncompliant)–Very few measures were in place to implement transparency obligations in relation to parties to trust and other legal arrangements. | Largely Compliant | Sri Lanka has addressed most of the deficiencies identified in the mutual evaluation report (MER) by making amendments to the legal instruments relating to trusts. Some deficiencies still remain. |
| No. 26 | Regulations and supervision of financial institutions (initial rating: Partially compliant) - The MER found gaps with market entry fit and proper, explicit prohibitions on shell banks, weaknesses in risk-based supervision, including supervisors reviewing risk profiles of sectors and individual enterprises or groups. | Remains Partially Compliant | Sri Lanka reported a number of points of progress with fit and proper with the insurance and securities sectors, but these have yet to come into force and there appear to be gaps in their scope. No information provided on progress with finance companies, authorized money changers and nonbank money or value transfer services (MVTS) providers |
| No. 28 | Regulation and supervision of DNFBPs (initial rating: Noncompliant) - Deficiencies noted in the MER included the operation of unlicensed casinos, no system in place for monitoring DNFBPs' anti-money laundering/ counter-terror financing (AML/ CTF) compliance, and no designated supervisor for DNFBPs. | Partially Compliant | Sri Lanka has made important progress with risk-based regulation and supervision of some DNFBP sectors; however, casinos remain outside of the framework for market entry fit and proper controls or AML/ CTF supervision. Real estate agents, identified as high-risk, are not licensed or registered and are not subject to market entry fit and proper. The Financial Intelligence Unit (FIU) has greatly enhanced its supervisory capacity and the conduct of risk-based supervision, including enforcement action. |

*continued on next page*

*Table 13  continued*

| Recommendation No. | Details of Recommendation | Rating Given | Reasoning Provided |
|---|---|---|---|
| No. 37 | Mutual legal assistance (initial rating: Partially compliant)–The Mutual Assistance in Criminal Matters Act (MACMA) did not provide for the application of its provisions on the basis of reciprocity and the range of assistance that may require use of coercive powers only available under the MACMA to prescribed Commonwealth countries and specified countries with which Sri Lanka had an agreement. It lacked a comprehensive case management system with standard procedures, accountability and clear time lines for handling mutual legal assistance (MLA). | Compliant | Sri Lanka's 2018 amendments of the MACMA addressed the identified deficiencies. The amendments allow Sri Lanka to provide MLA on the basis of reciprocity, provide clear responsibilities and accountabilities for processing incoming and outgoing requests, and require confidentiality for officers working on MLA requests. Sri Lanka has also established a case management system with standard procedures, accountability, and clear timelines for handling MLA cases. |
| No. 38 | Mutual legal assistance: Freezing and confiscation (initial rating: Partially compliant) - The MACMA did not provide for the application of its provisions on the basis of reciprocity. Assistance in identifying, locating, or assessing the value of property, and possibly freezing and confiscation, did not extend to instrumentalities intended for use and property of corresponding value. There was insufficient clarity in relation to the ambit of the provisions in the MACMA for asset tracing, freezing, and confiscation. Provisions in the MACMA for asset tracing, freezing, and confiscation were not broad enough to cover a wide range of foreign orders. | Largely Compliant | Important legislative changes to the MACMA in 2018 give a clear legal basis for Sri Lanka to take expeditious action in response to requests by foreign countries to identify, freeze, seize, or confiscate the widest range of property. This should be given particular weight. Sri Lanka has begun to support implementation of elements of asset sharing, and it is clear that there are no legal restrictions in relation to sharing of confiscated assets when confiscation is a result of coordinated law enforcement action. |

Source: Authors.

# 5 SUMMARY OF FINDINGS AND RECOMMENDATIONS

## Corporate Governance Frameworks

Corporate governance frameworks in South Asia have undergone a process of comprehensive modernization over recent years. In all member countries of the South Asian Association for Regional Cooperation (SAARC), except Afghanistan, Bhutan, and Nepal, corporate governance codes have been adopted. The codes are generally comparable to internationally accepted standards of best practice in corporate governance, although they are less demanding in a number of important respects, in particular the following:

- Codes generally do not require a majority of directors, including the chair, to be independent nonexecutive directors.
- Independence is defined more leniently or in general terms and, critically, often does not include independence from inside (i.e., large, but not necessarily majority) shareholders.

Where corporate governance rules are not nonbinding best practice standards, but binding rules, for example, because they are promulgated as part of the listing rules, it is critical that institutional capacity is adequate. In particular, regulators must be well resourced, the sanctioning regime must be appropriate, and employees must be well trained and appropriately incentivized to enforce regulatory requirements without bias.

Further, corporate governance standards will only work well if they are embedded in a binding legal environment that provides for effective investor protection mechanisms. The two main shortcomings in the surveyed countries are: first, the lack of an effective regime regulating related-party transactions and, second, a low level of private enforcement of company law by minority shareholders. Related-party transactions should be subject to review by a truly independent, well-informed entity, which may be an appropriately constituted board of directors or, for transactions exceeding a certain threshold, disinterested shareholders (approval by a "majority of the minority"). Legal systems should also include a modern derivative action mechanism that facilitates access to justice by allowing any shareholder holding one share or more to bring an action, with the reasonable costs of the proceedings borne by the company.

# Board Structure, Board Independence, and Board Diversity

The structure and composition of the board of directors is key for a corporate governance system to work effectively. The reason is that the board is the highest decision-making body, with owners and society entrusting it to manage the firm well and on their behalf. But corporate governance is more than just boards, with boards being the most important day-to-day mechanism. Other important dimensions are owners (type and structure), incentive structures, and company law.

Much of the research in this area focuses on board independence, a concept that has been widely adopted across South Asia, but with a very distinct own flavor. This report gives practical guidance on the role and function of the chair, as he or she is key in setting the tone from the top, and giving the right impulses. Another key dimension is board diversity. Typically, diversity is readily associated with gender diversity, but equally important is diversity of backgrounds, experiences, and opinions. A broad spectrum of opinions will make a difference in improving the quality of decision-making.

The issue is that (gender) diversity levels are woefully low across boards in SAARC countries, something that is important to address. One by-product of higher diversity levels is that better gender ratio typically improves the independence ratio, having a double positive effect on the organization.

# State-Owned Enterprises

State-owned enterprises (SOEs) in South Asia typically underperform the private sector heavily, and there is a perception that SOEs are generally inefficient and lack effective oversight and governance structures. A comparison of national regimes with the OECD Guidelines on Corporate Governance of State-Owned Enterprises shows that current national corporate governance structures fall short along most dimensions identified as critical by the OECD guidelines, and there is an urgent need for reform. Most importantly, surveyed countries do not use a centralized holding structure or a uniform regulatory framework to govern SOEs. Governance standards, where they have been drafted specifically for SOEs, do not always take account of the particularities of the SOE sector. The effectiveness of control mechanisms is often further hampered by human resources constraints and a lack of technical expertise. In order to tackle these issues, this report recommends:

Clear channels of accountability and responsibility for oversight of SOEs should be established. There should be one public body in charge of oversight and maintaining high corporate governance standards. The multiplication of reporting channels and overlapping control, appointment, and veto or approval rights should be avoided.

All SOEs that operate on commercial terms should be subject to one set of rules and legal requirements. General directors' duties and other general legal requirements should apply to boards of SOEs. Governments may produce a set of corporate governance rules specifically applicable to SOEs. However, these rules should apply without exception to all commercially operating SOEs, and their implementation should be supervised effectively, in order to ensure a level playing field and avoid confusion about the legal duties and obligations that govern the conduct of directors and officers.

Political intervention in the day-to-day operations of SOEs should be limited through binding legal and/or structural safeguards, for example, the interposition of a holding company that exercises all ownership functions of the state. Regulation should be put in place to ensure a high level of professionalism at the board and senior management level of the holding company.

Laws or a legally binding agreement between the government and the holding company should provide for a majority of private sector individuals with professional experience on the board of the holding company, and clearly delineate the instances when, and the processes through which, the government is entitled to intervene in management matters. At the level of the portfolio company, regulation, for example, a code of corporate governance for SOEs should ensure that SOEs are run in a commercially efficient manner and in the best interest of the company and its shareholders.

Institutional capacity should be enhanced at the level of both the enterprise and the holding company or other public body discharging oversight and ownership functions. At the level of the enterprise, it is necessary to enhance the professionalism of those responsible for internal management and control systems, awareness of the different roles, responsibilities and legal duties of executive and nonexecutive directors, and compliance with reporting requirements and other legal obligations. At the level of the holding company or other responsible public body, it is necessary to embed a commercial approach and ensure that those with the authority to take decisions concerning the management and governance of portfolio companies have the necessary technical knowledge and are familiar with the relevant legal rules determining decisions at that level.

## Compliance and Anti-money Laundering

Compliance serves as a key function to translate the understanding of risk into effective mitigation strategies. While compliance is often treated by organizations as a box-ticking exercise that does not add value, it is key to helping reduce risk in complex systems. Reducing risk is a very effective—and underappreciated—way of creating value in organizations. It is also essential for running sophisticated processes, and hence a modern firm.

Compliance is applied through anti-money laundering and counter-terror financing (AML/CTF) processes. Over the last 30 years a global AML/CTF standard has been developed that has resulted in the Financial Action Task Force (FATF) principles. While most countries have adopted them by now, some countries are still struggling to build up the necessary legal and institutional infrastructure. One main issue is that banks are free to interpret these principles, leading at times to inconsistent treatment. In addition, questions remain about the effectiveness of the various rules and procedures.

Going forward, this report recommends making the system faster and cost-effective, which can be achieved through migrating manual processes to digital systems—summarized as *"standardize, integrate, and automate."* It is important to standardize data collection within banks, and across banks in one country. Ideally, this initiative is coordinated across the region (*integration*), so data can be shared at the local and regional levels. Ideally, there should also be data exchange with government institutions,[156] beyond typical information exchange. Lastly and the most important step, the detection mechanism is then automated by using available *big data*.

---

[156]    A meaningful exchange is possible even without sharing identifiable information.

# APPENDIX
# SELECTED INDIAN LAWS AND REGULATIONS

In the following we provide the Indian laws and regulation on selected topics as a reference, given that India is both the largest country and economy in the South Asia region.

**Table A.1: Board Structure Regulation in India**

| Dimension | Regulatory Requirements Applicable to Listed Companies | Summary |
|---|---|---|
| Proportion of nonexecutive directors | s. 17(1)(a) Listing Obligations and Disclosure Requirements Regulation (LODR): The board of directors shall have an optimum combination of executive and nonexecutive directors with at least one female director and not less than 50% of the board of directors shall comprise of nonexecutive directors.<br>Top 500 listed companies are required to have at least one independent female director by 1 April 2019, and top 1000 listed companies must have at least one independent female director by 1 April 2020. | 50% |
| Number of independent directors | s. 149(4) Companies Act 2013: Every listed public company shall have at least one-third of the total number of directors as independent directors and the central government may prescribe the minimum number of independent directors in case of any class or classes of public companies.<br>s. 17(1)(b) LODR: Where the chair of the board of directors is a nonexecutive director, at least one-third of the board of directors shall comprise of independent directors and where the listed entity does not have a regular nonexecutive chair, or the nonexecutive chair is a promoter of the company or related to a promoter, at least half of the board of directors shall comprise of independent directors. | One-third if nonexecutive chair, otherwise one-half |
| Definition of independence | According to s. 16(1)(b) LODR, a director is only independent if:<br>• The director is, in the opinion of the board of directors, a person of integrity and possesses relevant expertise and experience.<br>• The director is or was not a promoter of the company.[1]<br>• The director is not related to promoters or directors in the company.<br>• The director has or had no material pecuniary relationship with the company during the current and the two immediately preceding financial years (apart from receiving director's remuneration).<br>• None of the director's relatives has or had a pecuniary relationship or entered into a transaction with the company amounting to 2% or more of its gross turnover or total income or `500,000 during the current and the two immediately preceding financial years. | Detailed and demanding definition |

*continued on next page*

*Table A.1  continued*

| Dimension | Regulatory Requirements Applicable to Listed Companies | Summary |
|---|---|---|
| | • Neither the director nor a relative of the director:<br>  – holds a key **managerial position** or has been an **employee** of the company in any of the three financial years immediately preceding the financial year in which he or she is proposed to be appointed;<br>  – has been an employee or proprietor or a partner of (i) the company's **auditor** or (ii) a **legal or consulting firm** that had any transaction with the company amounting to 10% or more of the gross turnover of the firm in any of the three financial years immediately preceding the financial year in which he or she is proposed to be appointed;<br>  – holds together with relatives **2% or more of the total voting power** of the company;<br>  – is a chief executive or director of any **nonprofit organization** that receives 25% or more of its receipts from the company or that holds 2% or more of the total voting power of the company; and<br>  – is a **material supplier**, service provider, or customer or a lessor or lessee of the company.<br>• The director is not less than **21 years of age**;<br>• The director is not a non-independent director of another company on the board of which any non-independent director of the listed entity is an independent director (**cross-directorships**)<br>A similar definition is contained in s. 149(6) Companies Act, 2013 | |
| Separation of chair and chief executive officer (CEO) | s. 203(1) Companies Act, 2013 prohibits companies from appointing the same person as chair of the board and managing director or CEO. However, s. 203(1) allows companies to provide otherwise in the articles of association.<br>s. 17(1B) LODR: With effect from 1 April 2020, the top 500 listed companies are required to ensure that the chair of the board is a nonexecutive director and not related managing director or CEO of the company, unless the company does not have any identifiable promoters as per the shareholding pattern filed with stock exchanges | Generally required, but exceptions in articles permitted |
| Committee structure | **Succession planning:** s. 178 Companies Act, 2013 requires listed companies to establish a nomination and remuneration committee consisting of three or more nonexecutive directors, not less than one-half of them being independent.<br>s. 19 LODR imposes similar standards.<br>**Audit:** s. 177 Companies Act, 2013 requires listed companies to establish an audit committee consisting of a minimum of three directors, with independent directors forming a majority. Further, the Companies Act requires a majority of the members of the audit committee, including the chair, to be persons with the ability to read and understand financial statements.<br>s. 18 LODR imposes similar, but more demanding standards. According to s. 18, two-thirds of the members of the audit committee must be independent directors, all members must be financially literate, and at least one of them must have accounting or related financial management expertise.<br>**Remuneration:** see above, succession planning | Nomination: yes<br>Audit: yes<br>Remuneration: yes |
| Enforcement | Binding on listed companies (with certain exceptions applicable, especially, to small and medium-sized enterprises (SMEs), see s. 15(2) LODR) | Compliance mandatory |

Note:

[1] For purposes of the whole section, the company includes a holding company, subsidiary, or associate company.

Source: Authors.

**Table A.2: Board Structure, Board Independence, and Board Diversity in India**

| Item | India |
|---|---|
| Framework provided by | The Companies Act 2013 (Act)<br>Securities and Exchange Board of India (SEBI) Listing Obligations and Disclosure Requirements Regulation 2015 (LODR) |
| Proportion of nonexecutive to executive directors on board | Rule 17 of the LODR provides that the minimum percentage of nonexecutive directors on the board shall be 50% |
| Number of independent directors | Section 149(4) of the Act provides that every public listed company shall have at one-third independent directors, of the total number of the directors in the board of directors (BOD) |
| Definition of independence | Definition provides in Section 149(6) of the Act |
| Separation of role of chair of BOD and chief executive officer (CEO) | The proviso to Section 203(1) of the Act and the Rule 17 of the LODR[1] provide, with certain exemption made therein, that the role of CEO and chair of the board to be separate. |
| Committees of the board | **Succession Planning**<br>No requirement stipulated for such a committee to be formed.<br>**Internal controls and the appointment/supervision of the external auditor**<br>Sec. 177 of the Act requires the creation of an Audit Committee and Sec. 138 provide for the appointment of an internal auditor by a company. However, the appointment of the external auditor shall be done by the annual general meeting (Section 139).<br>**Executive remuneration** Section 178 of the Act mandates the creation of a Nomination and Remuneration and Stakeholders Relationship Committee with three or more nonexecutive directors (Section 178[1]) which has the responsibility to "formulate the criteria for determining qualifications, positive attributes and independence of a director and recommend to the Board a policy, relating to the remuneration for the directors, key managerial positions and other employees" (Section 178[3]). |
| Board diversity | Rule 4(2)(f)(ii) of the LODR requires diversity to be factor when nominations to the BOD are being made.<br>However, the Companies (Appointment and Qualifications of Director) Rules 2014, by virtue of Rule 3, provides that every listed company and every company with paid-up share capital of ₹1 billion or turnover of ₹3 billion shall appoint at least one female director.<br>Further, Clause 49 of the Equity Listing Agreement requires the board of a listed company to have at least one female director. |

Note:
[1] As it was amended by SEBI (Listing Obligations and Disclosure Requirements) (Amendment) Regulations 2018.
Source: Authors.

# Compliance and Anti-money Laundering

### India and FATF

India is a member of both the Financial Action Task Force (FATF) and the Asia/Pacific Group on Money Laundering (APG). It became a member of the APG in March 1998, and a member of the FATF in June 2010. A Mutual Evaluation Report, which was published in 2010, was followed by a Follow-up Report, published in June 2013. The Follow-up Report noted that India had made sufficient progress for all of the core or key recommendations to render it removed from the follow-up progress. Since then, no follow-up has been done on India's initiatives regarding money laundering and terror financing.

### Legislation regarding AML/CTF and State Institutions Empowered with Supervision

Legislation/Regulations/Guidelines

#### *Prevention of Money Laundering Act 2002*

The Prevention of Money Laundering Act (PMLA) 2002 is India's premier legal instrument for tackling money laundering. It was enacted *"following the adoption of the Political Declaration and Global Programme of Action by the United Nations General Assembly."*[157] Sec. 3 of the PMLA 2002 makes money laundering an offense, providing that:

"Whosoever directly or indirectly attempts to indulge or knowingly assists or knowingly is a party or is actually involved in any process or activity connected with the proceeds of crime including its concealment, possession, acquisition or use and projecting or claiming it as untainted property shall be guilty of offence of money-laundering.

Explanation.—For the removal of doubts, it is hereby clarified that,—

  (i)   a person shall be guilty of offence of money-laundering if such person is found to have directly or indirectly attempted to indulge or knowingly assisted or knowingly is a party or is actually involved in one or more of the following processes or activities connected with proceeds of crime, namely:—
      a. concealment; or
      b. possession; or
      c. acquisition; or
      d. use; or
      e. projecting as untainted property; or
      f. claiming as untainted property, in any manner whatsoever.

  (ii)   the process or activity connected with proceeds of crime is a continuing activity and continues till such time a person is directly or indirectly enjoying the proceeds of crime by its concealment or possession or acquisition or use or projecting it as untainted property or claiming it as untainted property in any manner whatsoever."

---

[157] https://gettingthedealthrough.com/area/50/jurisdiction/13/anti-money-laundering-india/.

PMLA 2002 also provides for the seizure, attachment, and retention of property related to money laundering, by virtue of Sec. 5.

Schedule to the PMLA 2002, in Part A and C, provides a list of offenses, the proceeds of which are liable under the provisions of this act, as well i.e., Sec. 4.

### Unlawful Activities (Prevention) Act

The Unlawful Activities (Prevention) Act (UAPA) 1967, provides provisions making terror financing illegal and a crime. Offenses under the UAPA are included as predicate offences under the PMLA 2002.[158] Sec. 21 of the UAPA 1967 makes it an offense to hold proceeds of terrorism. Sec. 11, read with Sec. 3 and Sec. 7 of the UAPA 1967, provides penalties for dealing with funds of an unlawful association. Sec. 17 makes it an offense to raise funds for a terrorist act. Sec. 39 and Sec. 40 make it an offense to give support to a terrorist organization, and raise funds for a terrorist organization, respectively.

UAPA 1967 also provides for offenses committed by companies and institutions. UAPA also has an entire chapter that deals with the seizure and forfeiture of any property linked to terrorism.

## Institutions

### Financial Intelligence Unit

The Financial Intelligence Unit (FIU) is India's central, national agency for the purposes of anti-money laundering/counter-terror financing (AML/CTF), established by the government in 2004. It is tasked with receiving, processing, analyzing, and disseminating information relating to suspect financial transactions.

*"FIU-IND has set three strategic objectives in order to achieve its mission:*

- *Combating money laundering, financing of terrorism and other economic offenses.*
- *Deterring money laundering and financing of terrorism.*
- *Building and strengthening organizational capacity."*[159]

Imperatively, FIU is not an investigative authority, but rather is an administrative one. However, the director of the FIU, pursuant of Sec. 12 of the PMLA 2002, can inquire into whether a reporting entity (financial institution which had to report all suspicious transactions to FIU) is meeting its obligations or not.

The FIU publishes detailed yearly reports which map out the country's AML/CTF regime, and also contains vital information including the performance of the FIU over the past year. The FIU also releases brochures providing useful and vital information to relevant financial and nonfinancial institutions regarding their AML/CTF obligations.

---

[158]  Unlawful Activities (Prevention) Act (UAPA) 1967, Paragraph 4, Part A, Schedule.
[159]  Financial Intelligence Unit-India. Annual Report 2017–2018, p.3. https://fiuindia.gov.in/pdfs/downloads/AnnualReport2017-18.pdf.

*Directorate of Enforcement*

The Directorate of Enforcement, which comes under the ambit of Department of Revenue, is "responsible for enforcement of...certain provisions under the Prevention of Money Laundering Act. Work related to investigation and prosecution of cases under PML has been entrusted to the Enforcement Directorate."[160]

Its functions also include "search, seizure, arrest, prosecution action, etc. against offender of PMLA offender."[161]

*Other Important institutions*

The Reserve Bank of India and the Securities and Exchange Commission of India issue guidelines regarding AML/CTF. These guidelines operate in order to strengthen the AML/CTF regime in India. The Indian government has also formed interagency committees—AML/CTF Regulatory Framework Committee, Casino Sector Assessment Committee, Beneficial Ownership Assessment Committee, and Non-Profit Organizations Sector Assessment Committee[162]—to allow for greater institutional efficiency and coordination. The Ministry of Finance, India has a 10-member FATF cell which is tasked with overseeing the implementation of the action plan for AML/CTF and the recommendations of the committees.[163]

*What do the reports say regarding the legal framework/ compliance with FATF recommendations?*

*Mutual Evaluation Report*

In June 2010, a mutual evaluation report (MER) was published, which evaluated India's initiatives regarding money "from a range of illegal activities committed within and outside the country, mainly drug trafficking; fraud, including counterfeiting of Indian currency; transnational organized crime; human trafficking; and corruption."[164]

The MER 2010 also stated that, "Economic crimes involving criminal conspiracy; cheating, criminal breach of trust; forgery of valuable security; will; using as genuine forged documents or electronic records and other crimes of forgery are manifestations of frauds. These criminal activities are amongst the major sources of money laundering, as investigated by the law enforcement agencies in India. The Directorate of Enforcement (ED) has been investigating various money laundering cases emanating from these offences. The cases investigated were related to the following offences: corporate frauds; forgery of documents for wrongful acquisition of assets, both moveable and immoveable; and counterfeit currency (footnote 8)."

The MER 2010 went on to note that, "...In case of domestic crimes, the most common money laundering methods are opening multiple bank accounts, intermingling criminal proceeds with assets of a legal origin, purchasing bank cheques against cash, and routing through complex legal structures.

---

[160]   Department of Revenue https://dor.gov.in/preventionofmoneylaundering/ed-enforcement-directorate.
[161]   Footnote 4.
[162]   Follow-up Report 2013, p. 7. http://www.apgml.org/members-and-observers/members/member-documents.aspx?m=061b3b1d-da47-42e2-9d95-338b292c9096.
[163]   Follow-up Report 2013, p. 8.
[164]   Mutual Evaluation Report 2010, p. 10. http://www.apgml.org/members-and-observers/members/member-documents.aspx?m=061b3b1d-da47-42e2-9d95-338b292c9096.

In the case of transnational organized crimes, the use of offshore corporations and trade-based money laundering are some of the methods used to disguise the criminal origin of the funds."[165]

In regard to terror financing, the MER 2010 observed as follows: "India continues to be a significant target for terrorist groups and has been the focus of numerous attacks. The bulk of terrorist activities have been orchestrated by groups and entities linked to the global Jihad with the support of external organizations including State and non-State actors. In addition, several domestic groups involved in separatism and terrorism are also active. There are no published figures of terrorist cells operating in the country (footnote 8)."

And stated that:

"India itself has identified the following threats as the major sources for terrorist financing:

  a. funds/resources from organizations outside India including foreign nonprofit organizations (NPOs);
  b. counterfeiting of currency;
  c. criminal activities including drug trafficking and extortion;
  d. use of formal channels and new payment methods.

Based on the results of the threat assessment, it can be stated that while the threat is high from the criminal activities listed under (a) and (b), which according to the Indian authorities relate essentially to external terrorist organizations; the threat emanating from (c) and (d) is perceived by the Indian authorities to be low."[166]

*Follow-Up Report 2013*
The last report by APG on India's AML/CTF initiatives was the Follow-up Report published in June 2013. The following table provides the information regarding the re-rating of certain core and key recommendations:

### Table A.3: Re-rating of Core and Key Recommendations—India

| Recommendation Detail | Previous Rating | Re-rating |
|---|---|---|
| No. 1 – Criminalizing money laundering | Partially compliant | Largely compliant |
| No. 5 – Customer due diligence | Partially compliant | Largely compliant |
| No. 13 – Suspicious transaction reporting | Partially compliant | Largely compliant |
| SR-II – Criminalizing terror financing | Partially compliant | Largely compliant |
| SR-IV – Suspicious transaction reporting | Partially compliant | Largely compliant |
| No. 3 – Confiscation and provisional measures | Partially compliant | Largely compliant |
| No. 23 – Regulation, supervision, and monitoring | Partially compliant | Largely compliant |
| No. 35 – Conventions | Partially compliant | Largely compliant |
| SR. I – Implement UN instruments | Partially compliant | Largely compliant |

*continued on next page*

[165] Mutual Evaluation Report 2010, p. 12.
[166] Mutual Evaluation Report 2010, p. 13.

*continued*

| Recommendation Detail | Previous Rating | Re-rating |
|---|---|---|
| No. 6 – Politically exposed persons | Partially compliant | Largely compliant |
| No. 12 – Designated nonfinancial businesses and professions (DNFBPs) | Noncompliant | Largely compliant |
| No. 16 – DNFBPs | Noncompliant | Not yet equivalent to largely compliant |
| No. 17 – Sanctions | Partially compliant | Largely compliant |
| No. 21 – Special attention for higher-risk countries | Partially compliant | Largely compliant |
| No. 24 – DNFBP: regulation, supervision, and monitoring | Noncompliant | Not yet equivalent to largely compliant |
| No. 33 – Legal persons–beneficial owners | Partially compliant | Remains at partially compliant |
| No. 34 – Legal arrangements–beneficial owners | Partially compliant | Remains at partially compliant |
| SR VIII – Nonprofit organizations | Noncompliant | Not yet equivalent to largely compliant |
| SR IX – Cross-border declaration and disclosure | Partially compliant | Largely compliant |

Source: Authors.

www.ingramcontent.com/pod-product-compliance
Lightning Source LLC
Chambersburg PA
CBHW050046220326
41599CB00045B/7305